# ANTICLINE

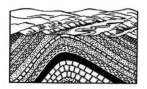

*Clayton Eshleman*

# ANTICLINE

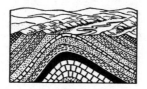

*Clayton Eshleman*

Foreword by Kenneth Warren

BLACK WIDOW PRESS
Boston, MA

Black Widow Press is an imprint of Commonwealth Books, Inc., Boston, MA. Distributed to the trade by NBN (National Book Network) throughout North America, Canada, and the U.K. All Black Widow Press books are printed on acid-free paper, and glued into bindings. Black Widow Press and its logo are registered trademarks of Commonwealth Books, Inc.

Joseph S. Phillips and Susan J. Wood, Ph.D, Publishers
www.blackwidowpress.com

Cover Design: Kerrie Kemperman
Typesetting: Kerrie Kemperman
Cover painting: Horst Haack, from his *Chronographie Terrestre* (work in progress), Panel 177, September 2002. www.horsthaack.com

ISBN-13: 978-0-9842640-6-3
ISBN-10: 098426406X

Library of Congress Cataloging-in-Publication Data on file

Eshleman, Clayton, 1935–

Printed in the United States
10 9 8 7 6 5 4 3 2 1

# ALSO BY CLAYTON ESHLEMAN

## POETRY

*Mexico & North* [1962]
*Indiana* [1969]
*Altars* [1971]
*Coils* [1973]
*The Gull Wall* [1975]
*What She Means* [1978]
*Hades in Manganese* [1981]
*Fracture* [1983]
*The Name Encanyoned River: Selected Poems 1960–1985* [1986]
*Hotel Cro-Magnon* [1989]
*Under World Arrest* [1994]
*From Scratch* [1998]
*My Devotion* [2004]
*An Alchemist with One Eye on Fire* [2006]
*Reciprocal Distillations* [2007]
*The Grindstone of Rapport* [2008]

## PROSE

*Antiphonal Swing: Selected Prose 1962–1987* [1989]
*Companion Spider: Essays* [2002]
*Juniper Fuse: Upper Paleolithic Imagination & the Construction of the Underworld* [2003]
*Archaic Design* [2007]

## JOURNALS AND ANTHOLOGIES

*Folio* [Bloomington, Indiana, 3 issues, 1959–1960]
*Quena* [Lima, Peru, 1 issue, edited, then suppressed by the
    North American Peruvian Cultural Institue, 1966]
*Caterpillar* [New York–Los Angeles, 20 issues, 1967–1973]
*A Caterpillar Anthology* [1971]
*Sulfur* [Pasadena–Los Angeles–Ypsilanti, 46 issues, 1981–2000]


## TRANSLATIONS

Pablo Neruda, *Residence on Earth* [1962]
César Vallejo, *The Complete Posthumous Poetry*
    (with José Rubia Barcia) [1978]
Aimé Césaire, *The Collected Poetry*
    (with Annette Smith) [1983]
Michel Deguy, *Given Giving* [1984]
Bernard Bador, *Sea Urchin Harakiri* [1986]
*Conductors of the Pit: Major Works by Rimbaud, Vallejo, Césaire,
    Artaud, & Holan* [1988, 2005]
Aimé Césaire, *Lyric & Narrative Poetry 1946–1982*
    (with Annette Smith) [1990]
César Vallejo, *Trilce* [1992, 2000]
Antonin Artaud, *Watchfiends & Rack Screams*
    (with Bernard Bador) [1995]
Aimé Césaire, *Notebook of a Return to the Native Land*
    (with Annette Smith) [2001]
César Vallejo, *The Complete Poetry* [2007]

# ACKNOWLEDGEMENTS

Many of these poems appeared, often in penultimate form, in the following magazines and blogs: *Electronic Poetry Review, Process, Jivin' Ladybug, Janus, New American Writing, Open Letter, Bombay Gin, Brooklyn Rail, Typo, ActionNow, Nomadics* blog, *Cannibal*, Jerome Rothenberg blog, *Bomb, Bookslut.com, Jacket, Denver Quarterly, Alligatorzine* (Belgium), *Mantis, House Organ, Gander Press Review, intervalles* (Belgium), *La Fovea, The Blue Jew Yorker, The Wolf* (England), Ron Silliman blog, *Scythe*, and *Parthenon West*.

"The Tjurunga" was first published in *The Grindstone of Rapport*, Black Widow Press, 2008.

*Hashigakari* with translations of the poem in French by Jean-Paul Auxeméry and Japanese by Takaomi Eda, was published by Tandem (Belgium)/Estepa in 2010. Two editions: 30 English/French and 30 English/Japanese, signed and numbered in a case (293 x 196 mm) with an etching by Matsutani.

*Eternity at Domme* (8 poems from *Anticline* originally written out in a notebook kept during a trip to France, June 2007), with translations of the poems in French by Jean-Paul Auxeméry, was published by Estepa Editions, Paris, 2010, with monotypes by Kate van Houten included, in a hand-bound, hard-bound edition of 200 signed and numbered copies (220 x 150 mm) on verge paper.

My gratitude to The Rockefeller Study Center at Bellagio, Italy, for a one month residency, autumn 2004, during which time I worked out the early drafts of "Tavern of the Scarlet Bagpipe." I also thank Harry Northrup, Ron Gottesman, and Christine Hume for their readings and commentaries on later drafts of this poem.

An asterisk by a poem's title refers to notes at the end of Sections I and III. Notes for Section II are not asterisked and are to be found at the end of the poems' Appendices.

# FOR CARYL

The California Institute of Technology biophysicist Max Delbrück once told an audience: "Men want to be praised; women want to be thanked." Dearest Caryl, I thank you *and* I praise you. You are the great companion of my life. You have made an immense contribution to my poetry and have offered me incomparable tenderness and love.

Of all the multiplicities that man sees and contemplates in the world beyond, those which delight, like houris, castles, gardens, green vegetation, and streams of running water—as well as their opposites— the horrifying kinds of which Hell is composed—none of these is extrinsic to him, to the very essence of his soul, none is distinct or separated from his own act of existing.

—Mulla Sadra

Poetry is multiplicity ground up & delivered in flames.

—Antonin Artaud

# TABLE OF CONTENTS

# FOREWORD

Tapping a metaphor from structural geology with *Anticline*, Clayton Eshleman evokes a natural framework for production that contains both gravitational points and nerve-centers connected to the down flow of art and poetry into his life. The associative power from the spatial metaphor suggests a concrete unity binds Eshleman's wildly looping self-referential stylizations to dynamic relations with image-rich environments, which span from the external world of caves and museums to the internal realm of dreams and fantasies.

Since the sixties Eshleman has been responding at the deepest threshold of personal arousal to insights from the psychoanalytic era. Drawing on Wilhelm Reich, Sandor Ferenczi, C.G. Jung, Norman O. Brown, Barbara G. Walker, and James Hillman, Eshleman belongs to an order of poets for whom millennia, the unconscious, and the depth of shamanic culture yield "the agility" to straddle signifier and soul. With *Anticline* Eshleman hazards a self-making end-time double plunge through living system and dying religion. In other words, *Anticline* is a book of autopoiesis and apocalypse. Within the fiery network of apocalyptic poets that includes William Blake, César Vallejo, Antonin Artaud and Charles Olson, Eshleman burns with the radical vision of human form that curves around rock and amplifies underground culture. In the name of rock, he enacts a Dionysian drama of depth that courts the feminine, ruptures misogyny, pushes back the language turn and remembers life brought into focus through the sixties countercultural revolution in consciousness.

From the outset, "The Tjurunga" positions Eshleman in a textured universe of human and symbolic relations with rock. "The Tjurunga" commissions the domain of tribal initiation and mythology to tell his story of self-creation in the spirit that makes a person whole. What "begins with a digging stick" unearths from chambers of memory the affective linkage and paradigmatic unfolding of mythopoetics in *Caterpillar*, the wonderful little magazine Eshleman edited in the late sixties and early seventies, which published in its first issue Robert Duncan's "Rites of Participation," an essay from *The H.D. Book*. Against the ever-enlarging context for understanding Eshleman's identification with the art of consciousness, the detailed notes he supplies to poems in *Anticline* support the powers of care, creativity and critique that have evolved through his lifelong practice. While Eshleman supplies an extensive note for understanding the poem in context, Duncan makes a point in the essay about "the primal identity of the person," a point that interacts to this day with the self-making produced in *Anticline*. Thus Duncan writes: "The tjurunga, like the cartouche that encircles the Pharoah's name as the course of the sun encircles the created world, is a drawing of the spirit being, an enclosure in which we see the primal identity of the person."

Nothing can be destroyed in "The Tjurunga," one of two poems which Eshleman regards as "the 'soulend' supports holding the rest of my poetry in place." With "a totemic cluster in which imagination / could replace Indianapolis," Eshleman thus marks the maw matrix of his autopoiesis:

> These nouns are also nodes in a constellation called
> Clayton's Tjurunga. The struts are threads
> in a web. There is a life blood flowing through
> these threads. *Coatlicue* flows into Bud Powell,
> César Vallejo into sub-incision. The bird-headed man
> floats right below
> 
> the pregnant spider

Eshleman's dismembered auto-production mobilizes proper names and referent relations onto the structure of the signified. In the process his "life" achieves "global positioning." In a note to the poem, he explains: "In my poem 'The Tjurunga' I propose a kind of complex mobile made up of the authors, mythological figures and acts, whose shifting combinations undermined and reoriented my life during my poetic apprenticeship in Kyoto in the early 1960s. At a remove now of some 45 years I see these forces also as a kind of GPS (global positioning system) constantly 'recalculating' as they closed and opened door after door."

Eshleman is a cartoon Überpoet, a maker and faker of his own grand referent. His constitution of the self through the wild nature of Dionysius suggests Nietzsche's influence. To be sure, Hillman's writings on initiation into Dionysian consciousness and feminine relational ground also provide psychological depth to Eshleman's dramatic self-stylization. With *Anticline*, Eshleman constructs a cartoonish portrait of himself as a manic poet hero who manages to "slip his mummy" in the abyss of the Great Mother. From "foreskin dinghies" to the jaguar of the Mayan *Popol Vuh*, Eshleman attunes himself to the dismembering that channels the black humor, cosmic laughter and semantic pull of a shamanic cut-up. In order to imagine reaching the Mother of Gods in the shadow of post-humanist thought, he must hypercharge Das Ding, thus floating the image of "foreskin dinghies in which poets travel." In the phallocentric aftermath, Das Ding is no longer possessed; it is sacrificed with a chuckle to the goddess of all things. While integrating left-over flesh into the language of shape-shifting discourse, the sacrifice attempts to rescue the plastic powers of the poet's subtle body.

Later in the book, when creative and destructive components for autopoiesis uncork from the political and religious imagination, Eshleman turns to the images of Hieronymus Bosch for retrospective revelations that might allow him to contain and contest the apocalyptic melodrama of his times. Accordingly he colors the tribulations of the George W. Bush presidency with the apocalyptic vectors of Kali and the Scarlet Woman in the hope a literal horizon of human rights might be revealed.

All told, Eshleman possesses in *Anticline* the mad capstones needed to construct a mythology of being that talks to the animals through Artaud's colon of unknowing. At the Cro-Magnon portal to animality, he feeds the Beast of the apocalyptic Christian conclusion the fruits of human imagination. Responding playfully to the germicidal impulses of the *Purell®* age, he declares boldly: "No god will disinfect the rock of my machine." Like Buddy Jesus turned thumbs down Antichrist, he generates through *Anticline* fresh hang-time on the cross of a signifying culture that crucifies human imagination. With "Pollock Pouring," his creative personality functions courageously in the crowded I of the psyche that incorporates "julienned white tapeworms" into the artistic burden of self-transformation. On the way to autopoiesis and apocalypse, he unveils himself through Pollock's persona, if only for the fun of it, the solar source of Hades finally "In the cunt of the Celestial Crocodile."


Kenneth Warren
Ransomville, New York, January 26, 2010

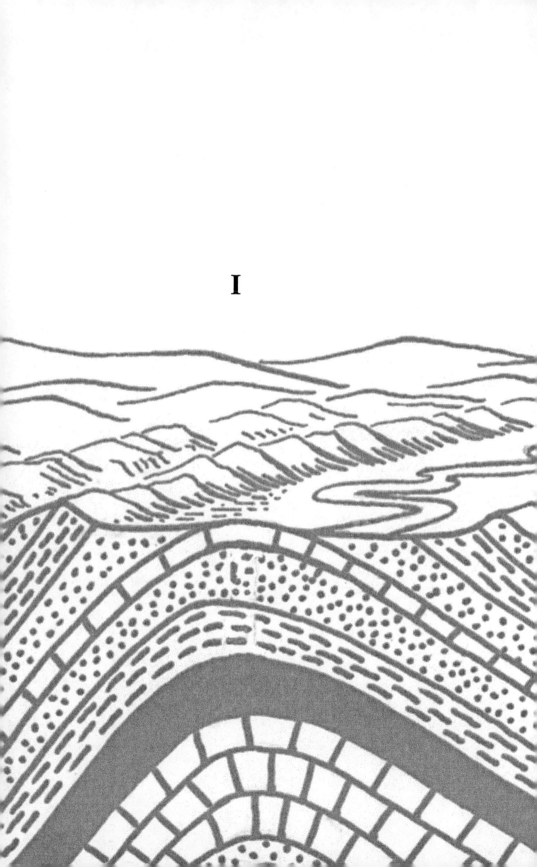

I

# THE TJURUNGA

begins as a digging stick, first thing the Aranda child picks up.
When he cries, he is said to be crying for
the tjurunga he lost
when he migrated into his mother.

Male elders later replace the mother with sub-incision.
The shaft of his penis slit, the boy incorporates his mother.

I had to create a totemic cluster in which imagination
could replace Indianapolis, to incorporate ancestor beings
who could give me the agility
—across the tjurunga spider's web—
to pick my way to her perilous center.

(So transformationally did she quiver,
        adorned with hearts and hands,
    cruciform, monumental,    *Coatlicue*
        understrapping fusion)

Theseus, a tiny male spider, enters a tri-level construction:
look down through the poem, you can see the labyrinth.
Look down through the labyrinth, you can see the web:

        *Coatlicue*

sub-incision      Bud Powell

    César Vallejo

      the bird-headed man

Like a mobile, this tjurunga shifts in the breeze,
                beaming at the tossing
foreskin dinghies in which poets travel.

These nouns are also nodes in a constellation called
Clayton's Tjurunga. The struts are threads
in a web. There is a life blood flowing through
these threads. *Coatlicue* flows into Bud Powell,
César Vallejo into sub-incision. The bird-headed man
   floats right below
                          the pregnant spider
              centered in the Tjurunga.


Psyche may have occurred, struck off
—as in flint-knapping—
an undifferentiated mental core.


My only weapon is a digging stick
the Aranda call *papa*. To think of father as a digging stick
strikes me as a good translation.


     The bird-headed man
is slanted under a disemboweled bison.
His erection tells me he's in flight. He drops
his bird-headed stick as he penetrates
  bison paradise.


The red sandstone hand lamp
abandoned below this proto-shaman
is engraved with vulvate chevrons—did it once flame
  from a primal sub-incision?


This is the oldest aspect of this tjurunga, its grip.


               Recalculating.


When I was six, my mother placed my hands on the keys.
At sixteen, I watched Bud Powell sweep my keys
into a small pile, then ignite them with "Tea for Two."
The dumb little armature of that tune
engulfed in improvisational glory
roared through my Presbyterian stasis.

"Cherokee"
"Un Poco Loco"
sank a depth charge into
   my soul-to-be.

This is a tjurunga positioning system.

We are now at the intersection of *Coatlicue*
and César Vallejo.

Squatting over the Kyoto benjo, 1963,
wanting to write, having to shit.

I discovered that I was in the position of Tlazoltéotl-Ixcuina.
But out of *her* crotch, a baby corn god pawed.

               Recalculating.

     Cave of
Tlazoltéotl-Ixcuina.
The shame of coming into being.
As if, while self-birthing,
I must eat filth.

I was crunched into a cul-de-sac I could destroy
only by destroying the self
that would not allow the poem to emerge.

Wearing my venom helmet, I dropped, as a *ronin,* to the pebbles,
and faced the porch of Vallejo's feudal estate.
The Spectre of Vallejo appeared, snake-headed, in a black robe.
With his fan he drew a target on my gut.

Who was it who sliced into the layers of wrath-
enwebbed memory in which the poem was trussed?

Exactly who unchained Yorunomado
from the Christian altar in Clayton's solar plexus?

The transformation of an ego strong enough to die
by an ego strong enough to live.

The undifferentiated is the great Yes
in which all eats all
and my spider wears a serpent skirt.

That altar. How old is it?
Might it cathect with the urn in which
the pregnant unwed girl Coatlicue was cut up and stuffed?
Out of that urn twin rattlesnakes ascend and freeze.
Their facing heads become the mask of masks.
*Coatlicue:* Aztec caduceus.
The phallic mother in the soul's crescendo.

But my wandering foreskin, will it ever reach shore?

Foreskin wandered out of Indianapolis. Saw a keyboard, cooked it in B
    Minor.
Bud walked out of a dream. Bud and Foreskin found a waterhole,
    swam.
Took out their teeth, made camp. Then left that place, came to
    Tenochtitlan.
After defecating, they made themselves headgear out of some hearts
    and lopped-off hands.
They noticed that their penises were dragging on the ground,
    performed sub-incision, lost lots of blood.
Bud cut Foreskin who then cut Bud.
They came to a river, across from which Kyoto sparkled in the night
    sky.
They wanted to cross, so constructed a vine bridge.
While they were crossing, the bridge became a thread in a vast web.
At its distant center, an immense red gonad, the Matriarch crouched,
    sending out saffron rays.
"I'll play Theseus," Bud said, "this will turn the Matriarch into a
    Minotaur."
"And I'll play Vallejo," Foreskin responded, "he's good at bleeding
    himself and turning into a dingo.
Together let's back on, farting flames."

The wily Minotaur, seeing a sputtering enigma approaching, pulled a
lever, shifting the tracks.

Foreskin and Bud found themselves in a roundhouse between
conception and absence.

They noticed that their headgear was hanging on a Guardian Ghost
boulder engraved with breasts snake-knotted across a pubis.

"A formidable barricade," said Bud. "To reach paradise, we must learn
how to dance this design."

The pubis part disappeared. Fingering his sub-incision, Bud played
"Dance of the Infidels."

Foreskin joined in, twirling his penis making bullroarer sounds.

The Guardian Ghost boulder roared: "WHO ARE YOU TWO THE
SURROGATES OF?"

Bud looked at Foreskin. Foreskin looked at Bud.

"Another fine mess you've gotten us into," they said in unison.

Then they heard the Guardian Ghost laughing. "Life is a joyous thing,"
she chuckled, "with maggots at the center."

# A TRANSMIGRALATION

I have César Vallejo positioned in my being.
I have turned him into my Spectre.
He now labors at my forge,
    flows through each containing wall, a bifurcating
maze,    filthy with unwashed adhesiveness.

What call this transmigration from one text
via translation into another,
the translator?  Is not the site of transfer a kind of *purgatorium*,
a place of cleansing?

On girders of black lightning black maggots are frying.

Psyche rises from the void. An elk is my Cro-Magnon mother.

The blow of creation at Chauvet: a 30,000 year old "minotaur"
hovering on a fang-like rock overhang
                            above
a fierce black vulva daubed there like a feedbag.
If they knew to hover this metempsychotic hybrid over a vulva
they probably had extraordinary semen fantasies,
possibly would have connected testes
via spinal marrow to the termite queen of the brain.

There's a pouch of menstrual blood & semen
attached to the back wall of imagination.
In it a rose mixture attempting to blend revelation
keeps singing *sukra ratka sukra ratka sukra ratka.*

March to this thunderstroke beat: God can only be tasted by angels.

Thus is there a sarcophagal taint in every hierarch.

The rootstalk of paradise is to be found in one's trouser-like tongue.

I am entombed in womb-like fortitude, expanded to curtailment.

[I began this transmigralation after having spent three days in the British Museum, April, 2007, having flown to London for the English "launch" of *The Complete Poetry of César Vallejo*. I had been reading & admiring Kristin Prevallet's *I, Afterlife*. Saturated with museum "afterlife," I realized that in the spirit that Blake's Los compelled his Spectre to work with him at the forge, with my 48 year translation saga completed, Vallejo's "afterlife" was (as far as I was concerned) to labor in my being. He was now part of my own intuitive machinery. Rather than cast him in the lake (as Blake elsewhere advises), I determined to include his cravings and revelations as implementations for my own "grindstone of rapport."]

Will man ever fall out of himself,
slip his mummy,
split his background,
discard his saviorial cartoon?

Never *is* oneself,
the astronomical amount of absence loaded into every conscious being.

Do all questions concerning the continuing existence of the soul
make up a constellation called "the afterlife?"

In the poem "He who will come has just passed," Vallejo implies that the resurrectional spirit of Christ, now neither of the past nor of the future but part of the air we breathe, is displayed in humankind's ontological contradictions.

6 AM. Caressing Caryl's cramped hand,
I see the two of us seated
facing outward like Egyptian King and Queen,
Caryl holding my head in her lap,
me holding Caryl's head in my lap.
Our faces calm, archaically smiling.

Behind this scene: Golgotha at full tilt.
Three loaded swaying crosses
surrounded by thousands, as at a 1905 Alabama lynch picnic.
I lock onto the eyes of one man in the crowd
staring voluptuously at the middle nailed man
—to realize that *He is Christ!*

Then who is that up on the cross?

"I am."

[for Kristin Prevallet]

## DEAR SIGN

April, 1979, patio of Marwan's house in mountains north of Alassio.
Rain—sunshine—snow the same afternoon.
Out to view the possibly-seeable ocean, some 10 miles away
(Caryl had just told me about Goethe's color theory).

    A cloud the size of a large, wispy shark
    zoomed down, away from its companion clouds,
    circled around us once,
    shot back up

vanishing in roily cloud wash...

According to Gary Snyder,
"Dōgen says: 'When the ten thousand things... advance and confirm
you, that is enlightenment. When *you* advance and confirm the ten
thousand things, that is delusion.'"

## ODE TO FELLINI

The man who really wanted to see
finally understood that he must sup blood
and sup it at the juncture of red jello and semen lagoon.
Jello because he had experienced broken placenta,
had watched one who had just given birth nearly die.
Jello because of the quiver, the hairline between being and
    stopping bleeding.

All this meant that he had to visit the spiders
and study the fairyland where madam dipped her chopsticks
    into her lover dinner,
then stood up on all four back legs and beckoned Bosch
    to restring the instruments,
for something new was starting up in hell:
the Bach in Cage, the ragtime in Powell, Nancarrow releasing
    arpeggios between cathedral and cantina.

There were now tongs draped in the web, sparklers set out.
Timorous crickets were inching forward.
A cicada with a broken bow (its leg) began to twang
and understand. As the blood piled out in rich pedestalian lobes,
the man who really wanted to see was all ointment,
a furry widower in a fake beatific get-up, nosing into
    the hose of his lady.

                What he tasted were cleats,
spiked heels strutting through the spider orders,
the nose of Odysseus, clipped by the Cyclops, planted as
    our maiden voyage.

There was never an immediate response, no response, in fact,
    as long as any system was embraced.
Catholic rage sweeps down the nave wearing a tottering crown of
    maggots.
Presbyterian anger doubles by the ikonless porch.
In the DMZ, Purgatory was glimpsable, horrific dividend,
    death cowled and sitting down for chess.

So it was nice to shift to a beach
with a terrier-faced whore, barking our hero on to a seaside grotto
where the honeyed mass could be lapped,
and the thighs of every other churned with the negation of the saints.
For the self is a dubious eraser glued to vanishing lead.
The well of the mother yields nothing, a nothing to be loved!
It yields and it yields, because—who are you?
              You are not always even something!
Sometimes: grasshopper on crutches, before a den of festive ants,
   each with a hardon bigger than both of your crutches!
Then it is good to sob hard against an antinomian window,
good to sit in the plexus of snow, reading your own shriveled paps.

# ABYSSAND

### I

The redbud, outside my workroom window is
but for a few pods, bare. As if
its skeleton now strides forth, essential armature.
I know better than to believe this.
The life of the tree is her full cycle.
To see her only in spring, only at the end of October,
is to project a male climacteric,
   rise versus fall,
         the duality that courses men.
True size is never visible.

### II

There is no other.
There is only the person I am not
  to be embraced in everyone.

So does identity loom in what I cannot grasp.
The invisible concurs. And the visible

which thought it was all.

### III

Our ends and the cowl of potential world end
throw ashen shafts into the faces of Orpheus and Eurydice
confronting each other at the brink of the organic world.

She is nun-like in contracted intensity.

He, gated by sunlight, smiles, knowing that every command of the
  gods who lathe us
is to be spun into fine furniture.

They are joists of our double-frame cohesion.

Nothing is absolutely dead.

IV

Dream in which I saw myself as an infant capering about,
the crown of my head still in my mother's vulva,
wearing her as if she were a nimbus, or cloud of light.

V

Deep in the mind's thermal, carnivorous dream ground
are cells in which jaguars are prancing.  The jaws of the oldest gods,
the bearded dragons, arched open. Out of these cuspidors,
skeletal geezers are ceaselessly squirming. They carry long knives.
They're on the lookout for baby jaguar gods.  These shades
still roam the Popol Vuh regions of the mind
where the Daughters of Xibalbá are ceaselessly
impregnated by spitting decapitated heads. Ceaselessly
bearing jaguar sons. Ceaselessly avenging, ceaselessly bearing,
coming into being while losing being, prancing
in the fumes from a massive caldron
                    brought to a boil by
                    earth's fiery core.

VI

The lesson of the 1980s was lesion.
North American society, discharging
the vitality in its colon, reassembled as Walmart,
Burger King. Spotting no end of purchase
it has dropped its load,   fled
in place
in sky
in dump.
Right, Frank Stella? Your metal technicolor bowel movements
    zig-zag museum walls.
Right, Vito Acconci? They pay to watch you crush a roach in your navel
    like Romans on a gladiatorial Sunday.

Sunday, that great arena of Christian excess
when church parking lots fill and pews receive
the gross weight of communion.
Perhaps you alone, smoldering
termite methane compost, contain our souls.

VII

Before I was born, I was already addressed and posted,
an amniota treading the whale music of the mother murmurs.

I could hear loads walking across her,
the heil spikes, the mush implicates.

I was a festering bubble mogul
tuned in to Placental Static in the chaos of my pillow.

I spent my infinity at the margin of the totally perishable.

Today every abyss invites me in.

VIII

          "Dear Lascaux," he began a letter,
"may I call you Las? Or Los? Every moment
you keep loosing and losing yourself in my works and days—
this is a miracle richer than Dylan Thomas's 'unending lightning.'
You continue to give out, give off, plumage,
an underground source spilling through Petrarch laurel and Laura,
fire source of a woman spread in labor, —turn her, crouch her,
point her *down,* so that her vulvic light spreads across
ant and forceps, bone and mildew,
                              the Sousa of a walnut's
branches asway in the otherwise rock junk radioed day."

IX

The transformation of mother into imagination versus her evasion
   in a quest for personal immortality.

Where death is in the hands of males, it is violent.

In the bay of mother, it is integral.

Without ugliness and horror at the base of a poetics, form and beauty
   are a sham.

Kali comes up the spinal holy dread of the poem as the sacred duality
   inherent in creation.

Without an appreciation of Her serpent power, the poem salutes
   the evasion of its freedom.

X

In autumn's arboreal emotions,
the carotid thrust is Kali, *rajas,* Absorber of all.

Ruddy Durgá-rich corduroy of leafscape,
amber violet dyes in harvest to
          the skeletal möbius
  strip
    tease of unclenching oak.

XII

But am I up to Kali? Will she deign to show me
life's full complement—
  the worm strumming in my palm
  Stigmata Sutra?

Vacuum is plenum
  abyss  bop
My Cro-Magnon grandmother
 a pulse of an artery away
    in gopher bone necklace
   arctic fox.


   XIII


Scarlet glossy ivy clinging to
the menstrual underskirts of Methodist brick


     *Brattleboro*


   XIV


Sunlit May day, the redbud going white, magenta
 sallowing out.
Soon, little green leaves, and my mind dripping with sermon.
*Via negativa* pours through,
weightless, insouciant,
carrying such yearning for weight as its wake.

The gone. A hollow in my seeing.


   XV


Rodin's sculpture proposes that psyche is never completely released,
never fully leaves the rock.
It manifests semi-submerged, caught in marble wave,
a Siren swarming
mantle.


   XVI


Down on my knees now, I'm talking to the octopuses
as one male, pebble by pebble,
starts again, from sea floor scratch,
to lay out Stonehenge.

XVII

As my sperm ghosts shred into
the fog of Ariadne's labyrinthine caress,
I am instilled with
the nothing trove of my emptiness.

XVIII

The horizon, with its eternity staves pulled out,
                                        stares back
with the force of a New Guinea mudman.

XIX

        The soul eats
from its own primal scene.
        As iguana
it clamps its mouth around the head of the turtle
    on whose back it is flexed.
Out of iguana turtle mesh our various faces flare
    "Behold now Behemoth which I
    made with thee"

Diesel monster of me on slave bone rails.

River of me packed in sand.

Oak in which I bleed roots.

Bottomless nail whose head I am.

[1989–2008]

Fortress of summer. Heat a connecting rod.
Black leaf mouth of the redbud chewing everywhichway.

Thoughts of George back in the hospital
so overwhelmed the light in those leaf jaws
I called Colette:
George was home,
                            difficult to speak, but he did,
courageous even, asking about Paul Blackburn.
"Where did his start?" Or more specifically: "Did it start
   in the esophagus?    I thought so…"

            Poetry, a nativity
                  poised
      on an excrement-flecked blade—

Paradise, you are wadding,
to plug one big gap?
                        Dogtown to be
so total a place in Charles Olson's desire
that concepts of hell, or any mountain-climbed heaven
become inadequate to the congruence of earth's facets.

But then there is the Celan-
hole, the no-one God, void of the ovens.

Dear George, I am moved by how many lives lived
are ivy.

By how life breaks through wall after wall only to provide
more stone.

How each is less than he is,
and more.

Self-knotted Nile of the anticline in which
we curl.

[9 July 1987–2008]

## AMBIVALENCE

    the cracks in
  everyone's coreboard.

During the late Beethoven Quartet this afternoon,
9/11 suicides leap from Bush's eyes.
Through bowels of clouds Rembrandt's elderly face appears
minor major focused:
compassion, carrousel and quagmire.

A furious washing of hands!
Water for Beethoven,
blood for the kneeling bells.
67 years as a fetus in
the womb of a bomb,
I'm a firefly
napalm gnome
(my psyche stuffed with forgetfulness gold.

[2002]

# CONSTERNATION I

I acknowledge the American government's infiltration of my psyche.
My mental atmosphere has become grainy, hyphenated,
cabbage-odored with seized distractions.
The bar TVs, on but silent, are mirrored in the bar's windows,
silting distraction through the heads of the talk-befuddled drinkers.
Maelstrom of a bar evening, thought cut with patriot-glare:
our leaders *can't* be clinically mad because such would mean
the nation is rogue? Or a war machine asylum?
Hardly an asylum, rather an arsenal in self-engorgement,
"Full Spectrum Dominance"

I am interested in automatic erasure.
I've read several times that Cuban exiles in Miami
carried out bombings in Havana, directed from Miami, in 1997,
& that since the early 1970s, the CIA has created weather modification
to ravage Cuba's sugar crop, & turned over to Cuban exiles
a virus which causes swine fever...
I read pretty well, but when I read information concerning
American terrorism, it doesn't stick—
I must reread it if I want to keep specifics.
I have ingested so much Americana in spite of myself
that it vacuums my brain, sucking up, into black holedom,
"negatives," making me study to remain articulate—

*"It's a freak show, David, I'm not here."*

Americana Logic 101:
"Let us live so well that we can give our government
permission to intervene, brutalize, & reap."

How deep is the Chosen People lode?
Do I write (as tough as it is to write coherently),
because it is less demanding than to press through political walls?

For what have I built this *House of Eshleman?*
For it to be shuffled & dealt out to those
who'll turn it over as *Ash Lemon Mouse?*

[Orono, 26 September 2002]

# TORTURE I

Corporal Merlin Herman all of whose body was burned
  except for his scalp.
The pain from his wounds.
The pain from associated trauma.
The pain cleaning his wounds.
The pain harvesting the skin, taking skin down to healthy tissue
  that has raw nerve endings.

Photo of an Arab in Guantánamo
in  bulky prison uniform, on his knees, attempting to pray.
His head is outfitted with sensory deprivation goggles,
a surgical-type mask, headphone-type ear coverings.

Blocking cell stem research today, Bush
proclaimed that he was saving lives.

[2006]

## CONSTERNATION II

Rumsfeld & Co do not experience the actuality of what they wish.
They glancify desks and reports, while the actual protocol
is the burnt black arm of an Iraqi 12 year old.
How close can I write to this dilemma?
Is it possible to express the hypnagogic power of
an unbombed American backyard
swelling into a red lake of news?
The ivy on neighbor Emily's brick has never been greener.
This is Bush & Cheney's most panicky hope:
that neighborhood sights will drown out
the killing splashing into our awareness.

[2005]

# TORTURE II

The American Abyss now a white 13 x 13 foot room with bash board
    on one side
so bodies can be smashed but the damage remain unobservable

This man has been pulped back into larval time
turned into a mask that can pass court inspection
he will never appear in court as they have not stripped him of
the mental architecture of his being
meaning he can talk
can expel his physical mentally-torqued stomach of misery

What does not change is the will to inflict pain
does Rumsfeld & Co know he is a farmer?
No matter
some are sacrificios to be drowned in the cenoté of Iraq linked to
    Al-Qaeda,
to feed the Burmese python of official American hunger for the
    relentless
tightening coils of the lightstick sodomizing
the anus fused doorwall of this Palestinian's agony

In the Name of the Father eradicate the Father
In the Name of the Son educate the son to see through the Son
In the Name of the Tortured break the grip of paranoia / domination
    basking in the testicles of government.

Lunch on deck with Marilyn Monroe. "Martinis for two" I called out, my voice light-headed with her Doctrine.

The horizon, now darkened by world-end fires, refused our advances. We were stuck, as if in two, in a century of black goals.

Mossadegh, Lumumba, Allende, Fadlallah, all "involuntarily administered suicides." "Four of over thirty," Marilyn quipped, "my Doctrine has become Atlas Paint covering the globe with Burger Kings & dipsomaniacal Queens. Have Americans no shame? When I bedded JFK I was embedded with our troops on Guam. Whose arm is this? I often asked the penis to the left. The Evangelical answer cartwheeled down."

Armageddon has become a kind of chess sparking dreams & fantasies in duel. Explosions & the deaths of millions torch this horizon, jamming all the signals from the 30 breasted Whore riding her Seahorse Hippo Wolverine. She's a lighthouse of sorts, raying out self-effulgence.

"And just what is the self?" Marilyn inquired, draining her vulva beaker once iced with gin.

Ah, the self, the engine of telluric clockwork & angelic overload which commands: return to your infantile all-is-God, secure in its pubic aviary. Shame is topless, or the Americans would have dropped to their knees after Hiroshima babes melted into shadow. The self is Hydra-potent, what one head learns, another climbs on. Such Siamese weddings produce rockets to the moon.

The astral earth buckles & breaks into a playing board rectored with disease crossbred with wealth. Gospel is everywhere ladled down into the seams of aboriginal integrity. "A third now always walks with us," Marilyn cooed, "one day it is Eliot with his lime rouge complexion dragging Tiresias by his dreadlocks. They're off, I'm told, for a tryst at the Ritz or by a campfire in Northern Arnhem Land. And if not TSE, well, a soul in a burnoose of fire whose skull has been riveted with pearls and iron."

Self-adhesion as being bound to one's fate, steeped in the fate of all each moment, is dangerously passé.

Fallujah under the blood map of a USA-shaped "thing." DU bombed city, hospital cots filled with stomach-exploded women, headless children, arms burned to black crust, fetuses like the contents of cracked eggs. The soaked rancid mattress, the doctor in despair, then shot by a marine sniper as he drives home to rest. Or the 15 year old scrounging the smoke-filled alley for something to eat, shot too. Iraqis soaking rice in dirty water, no fire at all or fire everywhere. Hospitals that look like Inquisitional vomitoriums.

The Beast free of its Whore rider, free to pillage, spread HIV, or to be blown apart by American 2000-pound bombs. Families boiled in their basements. Young women picked out by Hussein's terrible sons, raped, & when one complained, she was picked up again, stripped & covered with honey, then eaten by dogs.

Apocalypse of the male penetration, the archetype now so lethal it ramifies fucker faster to bunker-buster. What sounds like a cliché is the self infected with a replicating destruction genome, a phyloxera of the spirit, root louse boring into the foundations of all that is form. People sit stoned on violence giggling at joke-triggered applause. But the Joker, all smirk, is sprinting between the jokes, sewing, with his mayhem thread, mouth to mouth.

[2005]

## POEM BEGINNING WITH A QUESTION FROM
## CHARLES SIMIC'S REVIEW OF LOUISE GLUCK'S *AVERNO*     ★

"What was it to lie in bed with Hades surrounded
by corpses? What was on Persephone's mind?"

He broke through the bedrock, Hades
did, coiled in a narcissus as if awaiting my touch,
immediate narcosis... he was everywhere inside me,
a ghost fetal to every organ...
                              To be shanghaied
by the unknown, infiltrate of...    Is this
flower reverse?  Absence incubation?

My vagina...  his aurora wife to swarm...
sickened by the plunder of my sister pores...
prostrate before his manta loom...

Wafting chaff-like shades, their siloed mutterings...

Toad-sized flies have fecalized my mindstone...

I'm immortality's Sibyl husk...   for how many centuries,
                                        oh Demeter, will
His winding-sheet  be    stuffed in  my genital   shrine..."

# OF NANTUCKET IN A GRAVID LIGHT

A silence older than being.
A sound that has nothing to do with noise.

Anaximander's "apeiron"

Indeterminate potentiality.
Orison pulsing in all beings and events.

I am the lavender word, son of the arsinother,
daughter of the basilosaur.
I teach that each word is shredded with carnifex,
spongy, a capstone capping *sunyata*.

To play, as cello, the Grünewald Altarpiece.
To draw out its mole tones, its Sadean larvae.

Resurrection as fiber, not chain.
To master the mist machine, the belt of weightlessness,
the energy mace, to rattle my death scepter
as causeway, as call step.

Mind is a spectrum of dead reckonings.
What to apprehend in this fog?
Blake in his wave nest.
Dovetailing maelstrom accord.
Whale road become oil drum.
Blubber cut crucifix.

I still hear the terrible spermaceti thirst as
the Essex's black mate's chest is stove.

Poetry to admit in fugal trot:
the leakage into the past,
the leakage into the future, and
the whole range present as daily being non being.

The uprush of contradiction in my every veer.

Branchwork directionals. In relentless detour.

[for André Spears]

# HMMM

There is a hmmm, a hum, an incipient hymn, a
song in food, a hallelujah hint, even before
baby patter,   a Neanderthal lullaby,
suck of going in,   a sound,   a salsa
that sews me to you,
the sewing is thee,   we are
                    theed in sound,   treed in
        nascent omega.

I greet what I cannot account for,
I depart to where I might become an unfiltered phantom facing
    filtered war.
If sound is the heart noise of being,
does it have a commonwealth, a gong modality
    coursing our lives?

Cosmic lisp occurs most poignantly before falling asleep.
An oyster in shell-static, I hear a rapids spewing blood and gold—
*I am* again takes on flavor.

Breath's arsenal blooms in dreams.
Short of non-being, I pause to gaze at conception's regal tinsel,
its mire of mirrors, its tilting wetland bulrush miracles.

Breath molecules of the dead
populate the atmosphere, Adolph H as well as *ayahuasca*
comrades from the Putamayo.

The stuff Wilhelm Reich saw in the blue sky
looks like paperclips to me,
*bions* he called them, tiny soul packets
*on the verge*

or precipice where the living are shaved from the dead

or where the dead transfer
sprinting from one plane to another—

Blake bobbing by,
Beowulf, triple-eyed and forty-eared.

Hmmm. Deer can hear us talking. Our voices resemble the uh-huh of
falling fruit.

Did desire for reincarnation of the killed animal
preceed the notion of human immortality?

Hmmm. Like a sentient water molecule percolating randomly through
the soil, lost amidst the tangle of root fibers, I pass through the petiole
of a sun-drenched leaf… Now I am inside the domed roof of a
structure made up of lines—a rhizome.

Now I am a live canoe, my skin covered with yellow stripes, black
diamonds. Inside me are Sultan Muhammad, Pablo Amaringo, Unica
Zürn and César Vallejo. Crabs are clutched to my rear. They live as
parasites in the anal regions of large aquatic snakes. Zürn is pregnant
and twisting in pain. When Vallejo tries to soothe her, she bites off his
finger, which Amaringo puts in his pocket. Will he plant it? It is said
that the Yaje plant originated from a sowed finger.

Coreless core of the macro entwining the micro.

The quantum dot florescence image of a mouse kidney section.

Dream of green word leaves tumbling inside bright magenta filaments
in a royal
purple sky.
             Hertzog's blood-red black smoke over
burning Kuwait oil fields:  a kind of Beethoven bordello.

The seeker entwining the sought,
the sowed fighting to stay seed.

Caul of war, an American headdress for years to come.
As if what we are has become war birth,
the held-back fetus, our life, in a war womb.
When we sense birth, we are warforthed.

Sensation of living within a grimy welkin of unreality.
The dusk sky venereal with stealth.

In the nativity rip of the mind,
one wanders all one's roads at once.

## MEANOTHER

To slit open sin, to discover "face-before-birth,"
bog puss leather contracted into a nexus so stratigraphic
limestone and Mars pile into this vocabulary.

(Tough as cross hide, the Christ script conducted by an iced
    and antlered Satan).

I lifted my "face-before-birth" out of its vaginal loan,
the back of its head rich in salamander pigtails,
cutthroat eels, tubeworms that vibrate in methane seeps.

I moved into a soul pouch as if into a uniform of water—
Sweet Pea appeared, Veronica and Archie,
a flood of Toons wiggling like liquid termites.

To wear oneself as other, to hybridize
a single destiny into one that is multifoliate,
to envision the uroboric, to sense
bloodstream linkage as exterior congruence,
circular image causation feeding into / out of feeling,

        *meanother*

cutting through the representation shellac.

Yaw in roll with yaw,
the poem now tintinnabulates into auto-yabyum,
happy in its vulvic cap, a six-eyed imp,
madre succulent, Sweet Pea nosy, pater free.

# PLACENTA

Where is my placenta buried?
Must I know? After all, it is the globe of the origin of my soul.

Had I been a Kwakiutl, my parents might have exposed my placenta
so that ravens could eat it,
so that I might gain visionary powers in later life.

I dreamt that the first spot of land in the primal waters was a placenta,
a floating flat surface
attached to a long umbilical stem
anchored below.

Bodhisattva lotus throne—a sublimated placenta?

The Egyptian pharaoh was preceded in processions by
his actual placenta fixed to the end of a pole.
                    The first flag?

Are the hoardings of pack rats a placenta substitute?

Is the function of religion to keep humankind from becoming fully
    born?

## FULLY BORN

Megalithic Malta, a piece of flagstone
rising just above sea level,
a giant step from both Africa and Europe.

To roam the stone interior of these megalithic goddesses.
To stand on the vulva
road, inside seven foot
orthostats, breast
chambers…

Is my navel still my *Poteau mitan?*
Do I still rotate about it?
Paradise as a *walled* garden reverberates uterus.
To roam at will. If one part still meditates
inside, another part will become an immortality sucker.
Is dreaming the die in the ointment, nightly reminder
that psyche is a grindstone
ceaselessly crushing the nuts of the unrealized?

Only a faint hmmm left in this whelk.
The elliptical opening leads into a bulbous unseeability.
Staring into, a marine haze envelopes.
Vulva, first window.

Transformation of the novice shaman body—
the body so desired by the aged, ravaged Artaud.

Organs to be replaced by crystals, or sacred stones,
linked to an "immortal body"

answering a deep and ancient need.
"Now no one is in my tomb," the graduate shaman thinks.

Is he aware that his quest remains unfulfilled until
he kicks that no one out?

## LANGUAGE DEED

And you, mother, still without an afterlife
in the forms I generate—
                              drink with me
from the neck of this albino bat,
yes, and from the brain of this curving crayfish.
Right here to bear the fullness
and the rancidity
of life's doom and counter-doom.

A new horoscope buzzes with serpent-birds,
the vibration unfolds a nether-morn
through which, wearing a marigold shroud,
you wander. I am now a bison in the same moonlit tundra.
You are an avatar of Laussel.
I accept your facelessness as you wrench
from my head one of my horns,
                              a surrogate
for my phallus and for my heart. Held high:
matriarchal primacy. Nicked with thirteen notches.

Thank you for heralding my potency,
for not destroying my animalhood.

So, to be, in antic transformation. A window
in a serpent carriage. The wild cartilage of a shibboleth.
As if I were Petrarch revived at L'Isle-sur-la-Sorgue
(with Gustaf Sobin looking on) by my ghost lady
who, in womb, held my tongue-to-be,
her nestled little groom.

                    Against the pustular
core of the world the imagination thrives,
not by drinking there, but because it presses to
assimilate that mass.
                    I see you now,
as I could not on Acapulco's Caletilla Beach, 1959:

a jester skeleton in magenta Phrygian cap,
breaking in a gigantic green cicada,
having the time of your death.

Dream tonight of coupled images whirling
in the circus of an empty eye,
hurling themselves against themselves to become
under my lids a forest of magnetic needles.

        Everything is a door:
elephantiasis with its violet legs,
bougainvillaea's numberless magenta stars.

I opened to the pot-headed, lordly and deathless hybrids:

    chockablock
      animals and gods.
   O the breeze between! The shiver of
organs being lifted out! The emptied
      manger of the body filled
   with solidified light!

All the gods yet to be discovered will be found
on the night side of the blasted Tree of Life,
guarded by the black dragon of mindless unification.

    A sleepwalking sewer ringed with Aztec lime,
I descended to the point where the wind mangles eagles
and a three-legged toad contemplates
          an octopus clock's
      tentacle-tentative time.

      The hour rests
on a lake of charities.
No one ends at himself.

(Ideas ate the deities,
         the deities
became ideas,
      great bladders full of bile—

                    the sanctuary was a dung heap,
the dung heap a nursery
                            sprouting armed ideas,
                    ideas idiotic as deities)

We have caught up to Whitman. But his hand in mine
has the feel of a Sudanese infant's claw.

            There is no freedom.
There is only the intensification of
the sensing of *forever* as one lives *now*.

## DIA DE MUERTOS

Nora, Leon, Bill—I would be adrift with you in that dinghy
Bill painted off Bosch's *Ship of Fools*,
the four of us, as souls, with wine and watermelon,
our *ofrenda* between us, stacked burins, scrapers, brushes, notebooks

and, just to keep everything true to imagination,
a squirrel smoking a cigar. On our mast a tricolor would flap
so that Matisse's words *Travail et amour*, as on a mobius band,
would circulate within each of us. And our talk!

We would have finally gotten our whole lives into what we say.
Our conversation today, concerning *kalokagathia*,
or "the beauty and goodness of a consoling art," would spin out,

angel cradles between our gesturing hands and mouths.
Then it would be time for me to go. I would slip out, regain the shore,
and wave farewell to you, dearest friends, for another year by Caryl.

Without Caryl
how thingness looms,
pressed up against this Tavistock Hotel room,
place without aura.
                    The wallness in life
mostly backed off when I am with her.
Now I see the edge of the dead carpet,
the dead plastic phone
          in its cradle.
I am in the land of the still,
hand on crisp bed-sheet
—even it is strange
without her.
                    Returned to a time in my childhood
when I felt no human other. Sensation of listening
to my father beat Sparkie or Ginger
because they shat where they were not supposed to.

Mutual presence is a fluidity diminishing
    the thingness in life,
enabling mind to move as metaphor,
            making possible
          mental pleasure.


                                        [London, April 10–15, 2007]

# LUNCH WITH HERBERT

What is it to be in the presence of another?
To share air? We are friends because in each of us
there are inner parliaments on fire.
You've trimmed your fat—did you know
cannibals invented the fork?
We are fragments of a plural yet to be auditioned.
We see the world as men embedded in the petrification of a crisis.
Before our gaze: rungs of the ladder upon which
angels and devils scamper up and down.
Why is that angel carrying a skinned horse?
How can that devil climb and, at the same time, give birth?
The suicidal tension in the library where all the books
lie open to each other. Merge
but do not violate. Be vital with erosion,
self-aware in global space strafed by
daily annihilate news.
Consider the cubistic flexion of the knobs on
any spoken word, near-thoughts
like clustering fireflies damned up in eyes.
To acknowledge my friend by allowing him to enter
summation's *temenos* and not be cleaved there
or cried upon. The cost of honest unity
suspended over
the subconscious rage of others.

[29 April 07 / NYC]

Leon Golub, primarily smiling.
Or that is how he strikes me, as a soul now, gone and
present, a rugby of a soul, all bristle and scraping and delving into,
feisty Leon, writing funny letters to art critics
calling them in effect or literally assholes.
But we laughed much more than we growled,
for years, especially at 71st and Broadway,
Nancy making chicken dinners in the tiny kitchen
where the six of us sat at counter facing a wall,
then to range in the unfurnished main room, one big table, chairs,
a single work of art:
            an African crocodile head sculpted out of wood—

                            I am still amazed at how warm and
totally "furnished" that apartment seemed. Leon's anger
mixed with yelling and guffaw, his twang and his bottomless good
feeling for what was right about the world.
                            Vallejo
in his negativity is affirmative.  The engagement, its depth, and its
        desire,
makes the listener, or reader, feel right about being alive, or
so people tell me. Comes back looking at this photo of elderly
Golub smiling, which does not play false his relentless ripostes,

or last night smiling, convivial Ron Padgett with his darts
and thoughtful undercuts, yet comedic with the humor of experience.
I listen to him at my old university, he talks to the students,
afternoon lecture on collaboration, useful stuff, delivered with warmth.

## SIMPLE FRENCH FOOD

Thinking of Richard Olney, especially
this morning, walking the gym track
listening to Brahm's First Piano Concerto.
"Gratitude" is the word which kept coming in,
"grititude," as well, Olney as a beautiful
example of gratitude and grit,
the thousands of meals he cooked for friends at Sollies-Toucas,
the amount of imposition he put up with...
His *Reflections* is a testament to finding one's own way
then making that way count.
Gratitude to the bounty of the earth that enables some of us to live
as we do, gratitude
to those friends who come through.  Richard
in his kitchen, in rags (he called his clothes),
working through an alchemy of transformation from painter
    to cook to
food and wine scholar, taking so much shit from people like Georges
    Garin
but, once someone was a friend, not denying them invitation, or even
residence while Richard was away.

Think of what is happening to the earth:
in America's "cancer corridor," a 150 mile-long stretch of the
    Mississippi River
between Baton Rouge and New Orleans, city-sized chemical plants
    dump more than 50 millions of pounds of toxins annually.

Then I think of Richard Olney
who did not suffer fools,
who stuck by his sense of honesty/integrity.

I have been cooking out of his *Simple French Food* for 33 years.
My friends think I am a good cook.
I am. A good amateur one.
Most of what I know has come from Olney.

To cook tasty, nourishing food for friends. What a bounty.

[2008]

# THE LEFT FOOT OF KING RAMESSES I          *

resembles a long semi-flat black fish.
The toes crawl forth,
five black tent caterpillars on their way to a cherry tree feast.
From the tips of their abdomens they secrete pheromones
so that their relatives, detecting these chemical signals,
can also stream down the trail!

From Permian times onward, tent caterpillars have had no god.

When they reach a leaf patch at the end of a branch, they snuggle side
by side, humming and feeding in unison on a young leaf.

Many a tentstead is torn and littered by the shrunken cadavers of larvae
killed by braconid wasps.

Having detected the buzz of a tachnid's wings, a tent larva swings its
body from side to side in a kind of samba, creating a moving target,
befuddling the attacker.

Fully formed tent caterpillars chew their way out of eggs in sync with
their host tree's bursting buds.

They happily cooperate in many interactive tasks: leaf-shelter building,
communal basking and mat spinning, anti-predator group displays, trail
laying, recruitment to food and basking sites.

Tent caterpillars are at the pinnacle of caterpillar social evolution and
should never be dissed as "walking digestive tracks."

They have six eyes, which tragically provide them with no information
about the form of an object. However, by swinging their heads, they
perceive dark vertical shapes against light-colored backgrounds (much as
we would see branches against the sky).

They have color vision (ultraviolet light and shades of green); they use
the sun as a compass.

Successive cycles of body waves propel them forward, carrying along their sixteen legs.

A typical female may emerge, call males, copulate, lay eggs, and, completely spent, die in less than a day.

They love to feed on water tupelo, aspen, water oak, flowering dogwood, and cherry.

Their great epic, *The Cherry Tree Journey*, translated in 1530 by the blessed Persian angel Sorush, describes the journey of the Ortok tent caterpillar clan to retrieve the princess Zal carried away by a warbler and deposited in a bird-citadel in the top of a tall cherry tree.

Other enemies are beetles, stink bugs, ants, wasps, chickadees, titmice, bluejays, the Baltimore oriole, redwing blackbirds, chebecs, wood peewees, phoebes, cuckoos, downy woodpeckers, red-eyed vireos, and the brown-headed cowbird.

They have no known friends.

Think about this: any aggregate of birds or animals that cooperated to build communal shelters, shared information regarding the location of food patches, *and had their own epic,* would be considered a highly social unit.

Their sole musical instrument is thought to be the Cryptonephridium, embedded in the walls of their rectums.

It has recently been conjectured that the tectiforms engraved and painted on the sides of bison in the Upper Paleolithic cave of Font-de-Gaume may have been based on tent caterpillar shelters which may have inspired Cro-Magnon people to construct small hide-covered lodges.

The first architects!

We must now conclude this brief excursion by crawling back into the toes of Ramesses I's long black fish-foot, colonized with the rest of his statue in a glass case ("Mummy Section") of the British Museum.

## MATTERHORN, WESTERN FACE        *

Out of a small doorless plane, half hanging, Bradford Washburn, 1958,
in a cloud storm photographing the Matterhorn's southwest
—can we call it a "face"?  Of a snowy owl,
beak in petrified drain down between the torn-out eyes,
wearing a cloud storm peruke! "I am
      the unfathomable
upreach
        breaking off
midstride of heaven,
              havenless
   ice harpsichord,
           eroded
      primordial mound"

Voice of the self lodged in an eruption remainder?
Or the sound of anticlines, surge of imaginative
cresting as, at 73, on all sides
        entropy pulls down?

Apparition of this "meadow peak" as Kali
wearing a necklace with the skulls of Hadow, Croz, Hudson & Douglas,
voracious pyramid! Temple of duality!
Lingam gneiss upfolding out of oceanic crust
in which I open a yoni hole
      to the mountain's uterine altar:

flat, tall blade incised with runes resting on
two stubby appendages (like lopped off thighs)—
in the center a woman's groin,
the thigh stubs are also testicles,
yet this altar is fundamentally a female
whose torso and head have become ithyphallic,
as if the vulva self-erected,
        a hole
that grew into a pole,
        the hidden
as the realm of emptiness that radiates All—

guarded by a cross-eyed faun, whose round dance weaves
a labyrinth of confusion for the Pale Man,
eyeless, mouthless, arms flailing, staggering toward
but never reaching this tzimzum simu-
                    lacrum of the soul.

# DESCENT

> "Why do poets write vertically?"
> —Sam Shepard (after the
> Vallejo program)

Cremasteric
metaphor. Descent intensifies
consciousness.

Laddered
language rooms
        constructed,
then ransacked,
    each next

        a trap-door
nexus,
        each door
a downwind Pandora

opening into
the reversal of gravity:   to take my own time here,
brushed by ascending, descending angel
    breath.
        To pick my way
    down...

(The trail through Le Tuc d'Audoubert was marked by
strings tied to stalagmite stumps.
We could only crawl inside the string "aisle"
one by one. On each side of us,
 "virgin" ground    strewn with
viper skeletons, bear skulls.)

  As my body contorted
                in Le Tuc to
accommodate our "stanza path"

so does the line here
        versify (akin to *vertere,*
"to turn") when meaning
   shifts (specter of prose plowing
a rectangular field).

        Line beginning and end
words are out sides
up against the page equivalent of
            "virgin" ground.

Can the page blank be thought of
                as gnawing at
these stanza sides?  Are they
            stays against
the walls of voicelessness forever
   pressing in?

        Black road to Xibalbá.
   Cleft in the Milky Way.

Below closure's boneyard,
            Absence:

   source of the next

poem's being.

# READING LAURA SOLORZANO                                    *

Marinated in the brains of the mask
I dip into paralysis & flicker embarrassment,
pregnant as a just-rammed mare
                    watching the stable collapse,
leaving me eight-legged, a spider-inspired, equine jest.

You stare through the eye holes across a bridge
                    swarming with sonic
chromatic refugees, ewe-eyed yoyos,
intertwining escalators loaded with jasper
                    jerking to
the agon rays of amber ravenous trolls.

The brains of the mask: waterspout of the inseparable
interlocking of matter with its spiritual gist,
skeletal trumpet through which winds
the lamprey labia of our natal elation.

                At the head of the mother table
loaded with fruit      Death smashes eyes into his hands,
then staggers toward us as a glissando of asps
singing as they strike mirrors into our liver narcissus.

Up we go through the mask's trapdoor into the Hadal trench
behind the eye holes
275 miles north of Havana where lounges

a hammerhead shark

wearing Hart Crane's light topcoat.

I know something about the pressure you are under
having just returned from an abyssal brothel
where a cockatoo squidette instructed me in the moves
necessary
                    to inject energy into the anchor buried in your navel.

Sensing you as an icicle up the anus of Hell,
I am sending you a wagonload of what Anselm Kiefer calls
the first and oldest metals of alchemy—lead—
the least pure, the most ambiguous, Saturnian,
the ground zero of transmutation.

I am also sending you a Mousterian orchestra of mastodon
    skull drums painted with menstrual crosses,
cloud scores crisscrossed by lark arpeggios,
a nose flute from Les Trois Frères,
a Siberian hip-bone xylophone.

There is a black Moby Dick cruising America's white Hadal trenches,
    attached by Oglala Sioux hatchet fish.
There are black Eshlemans and white Alexanders exchanging
    fission in Aimé Césaire's coral arsenals.

We must ask the poem for the impossible, locate ourselves
within this asking, spot the Stone of Division,
then attaching ourselves to this Stone
articulate the amoebic split-off of the divine and the human.

The imagination is a primal hourglass of venusian sensuality,
a kind of double bellows ceaselessly troating
                    (in the words of Lezama Lima):
"Image is the reality of the invisible world."

A bison drops its human embryo into fiery snow.
Cro-Magnon eyes litter the rune-scape.
Rising through the tundra are rods of emptiness,
pedestals for meditating saints and poets,

ping pong balls hailing bop
over the luscious hiss of *sin and be.*

Why does the clock dial register 6:66 AM?
Is this a sign that the missing 80% of the cosmos is right around
   the ayahuasca bend? But wait—
I think I have spotted your gnarl in the rudimentary
   nipple of a bee. Or have I been hypnotized by Dionysus
            on his boar tusk harp chanting
        semen-honey lays?

Moaning in the eel-grass are your "oneiric sesame pontoons".
This eel-grass undulates in vertical homage to
         the light in your speech lattice,
      your holophrastic triadic units,
   your brobdingnagian vocabulary accessible in trance,
   your field mice parachuting between cat-pawed traps.

Nothing, as active subject—can we agree on that?
Can we love the soul in all its resurrexit end-blessed mess?
Can we imagine *Banisteriopsian* verbal ladders?

It is out of nothing that, through heat and compression,
we make our words. Our verbs! The hooligan equivalents of stars
—and the earth? The earth is a thaumaturgic enigma
still cooking inside, still being forged.

I am sending you as well some redbud pussy-willow rubies—
sew them, like eyeballs, to your back in the fashion of certain
   Maya underworld lords.
I am sending you an etymological halo,
a solar ghost-roamed threshing floor.
I am building for you a mask to strap on
                  when,
            suspended in the stroma,
your drum arrives walking on animal paws,
pregnant with intestinal tallow.

[December, 2007]

March 4, 2008, Los Angeles.
Antonin Artaud dead 60 years.
Sedna with thick pigtail growing out of one eye socket
watches over his seal body
bewitched into transmorgrifying forms.
Nkonde pierced, daggered with Christ lip needles
sewing a calvary of interlocking math.

Sedna weeps cisterns of rote lore, Inuit savoir-faire.
She offers the homuncular Artaud
a little sled of fox bones. Off he goes into
the heart of our anatomical dilemma:
there is no quartz body, there is only an imaginal corset
sheathing mortality-poisoned mind.

                    360°
view of a life, all of life all
at once. Childhood crater &
fetal Frankenstein. Grotesque because
whole. Carnival-layered. Mythically
dismissed. Contradiction's grindstone
braying fragmentary precisions. Is
paradise black? I thought it was lit by mother suns.
I thought paradise was mental war
in which contestation revises what mother conception
prepared us for. Insurgent, virulent Frankenfetus.
Tiny gold maggot of *I am.* Butterfly *we.* Monstrous
presence of Sedna, the mother
under Marseilles, she is
artichoke
choked anus of
the master pater who
ejaculates ass daily.
Where is Artaud now?
Under Inuit organs?
Freed of French Catholic trance?

*

Artaud cuts Sedna with his knife. She shrieks with joy,
delighted that he is cutting from her filthy body
the stillborn & the aborted.
"Now comb & braid my tresses," she croons,
while her tailless red watchdog barks scarlet bubbles.
Artaud cuts out her eye pigtail, releasing from the socket
the pre-sent present which he concertinas into
a cranial tree
so that the bark of the word is interior to
the capillary fistulae of
the brain's fugal pores.

The bodies of Artaud & Sedna merge,
A text of prancing ampersands, entrailexhalations.

*


Sedna's waterlogged shaft receives Artaud's bewitched eternality.
Black paradise of the fetus aviator womb.
Black paradise of the anarchic intrusion of the askew.
Joy of being a fetus in an archetype.
The humor in Artaud is a masque in which tarantulas
make wisecracks while being milked by kindly aphids.
O, the being in the goddess,
ripped from her rafters by walrus cops.
These are the songs of anti-experience, of the verbal jitter jig
caught from devouring the brains of the dead.
Artaud is nature uncast, an alligator-shaped man
purring like a demon slipper.

*


To remain on Sedna's vermiculate surface
as a brown cave spider: this is Antonin's wish.
Five miles south of Marseilles
(with its Artaud family graves,
a "hideous, pornographic" & stratifying Cross
etched in his), he travels through

the underwater shaft leading to the Cosquer cave,
henceforth to be known as *Sedna's Skull,* reached by
her long neck shaft
leading in from the Mediterranean.

Now physically porous as outer space,
he crawls her cranium's bell-shaped interior,
the primeval magma of meandering lines in which all beings
alive and imaginary merge.
With his paps he explores her moss animals,
her amber calcite streams,
the giant auks, the seals & jellyfish
glistening on her Urgonian mass.
Sedna's constellations. The unbelievable is the truth.
No peace in this universe called To Live.

[for Stephen Barber]

# NOTES

## The Tjurunga

I was first alerted to the *tjurunga* (or *churinga,* as it is also spelled) by Robert Duncan in his essay "Rites of Participation" (from *The H.D. Book*), which appeared in *Caterpillar* #1, 1967. Duncan quoted Geza Róheim ("The *tjurunga,* which symbolizes both the male and female genital organ, the primal scene and combined parent concept, the father and the mother, separation and reunion... represents both the path and the goal"), and then commented: "This *tjurunga* we begin to see not as the secret identity of the Aranda initiate but as our own Freudian identity, the conglomerate consciousness of the mind we share with Róheim... the simple *tjurunga* now appears to be no longer simple but the complex mobile that S. Giedion in *Mechanization Takes Command* saw as most embodying our contemporary experience: 'the whole construction is aerial and hovering as the nest of an insect'—a suspended system, so contrived that 'a draft of air or push of a hand will change the state of equilibrium and the interrelations of suspended elements... forming unpredictable, ever-changing constellations and so imparting to them the aspect of space-time.'"

Reading Barry Hill's *Broken Song / T.G.H. Strehlow and Aboriginal Possession* (Knopf, 2002) brought back and refocused Duncan's words.

In Vol. 13 of *The Collected Works,* para. 128, Jung writes: "*Churingas* may be boulders, or oblong stones artificially shaped and decorated, or oblong, flattened pieces of wood ornamented in the same way. They are used as cult instruments. The Australians and the Melanesians maintain that *churingas* come from the totem ancestor, that they are relics of his body or his activity, and are full of *arunquiltha* or mana. They are united with the ancestor's soul and with the spirits of all those who afterwards possess them...In order to 'charge' them, they are buried among the graves so that they can soak up the mana of the dead."

In my poem "The Tjurunga," I propose a kind of complex mobile made up of the authors, mythological figures and acts, whose shifting combinations undermined and reoriented my life during my poetic apprenticeship in Kyoto in the early 1960s. At a remove now of some 45 years I see these forces also as a kind of GPS (global positioning system) constantly "recalculating" as they closed and opened door after door.

In the thick of breakthroughs often interpreted by my confused mind as obstructions in Kyoto, I was able to complete only one poem that struck me as true to my situation and destiny as a poet: "The Book of Yorunomado." Thus I opened the poetry section of *The Grindstone of Rapport / A Clayton Eshleman Reader* (Black

Widow Press, 2008) with this poem and closed this section with "The Tjurunga." With bookends in mind, I see these two poems as the "soulend" supports holding the rest of my poetry in place. Thinking back to Vallejo pointing at my gut in 1963 and indicating that I was to commit seppuku, I was struck by the following quotation from James Hillman's *Animal Presences* (Spring Publications, 2008), p. 141: "The theological message of the Siva-Ganesha, father-son pattern can be summarized in this way: submit that you may be saved, be destroyed that you may be made whole. The sacrificial violence is not the tragic conclusion but the necessary beginning of a passage into a new order... the God who breaks you makes you; destruction and creating ultimately spring from the same source."

**A Transmigralation**

According to Northop Frye (*Fearful Symmetry,* Princeton University Press, 1969, the chapter titled "Nightmare With Her Ninefold"), the Spectre of Urthona, in "The Four Zoas," "properly controlled, is the obedient demon who brings to his master Los the fire and metals and other physical needs of culture, and brings the artist his technical skill."

The Spectre also "provides Los with a constant will which makes his vision consistent and purposeful..."

My initial sense of the Spectre of Vallejo in Kyoto, 1963, was that aspect of Vallejo which defied translation. Confronted with such resistance (in "The Book of Yorunomado"), my only solution was to destroy my given life for a creative one in the hope that such would enable me to overcome the resistance in Vallejo's poems, and to achieve a realized translation (of, at that time, *Poemas humanos*). At that point, then, my relationship with Vallejo became two-fold: "he" was a text to translate *and* a figure of resistance I had created, at that time, to overcome. However, this relationship extended way beyond the translation I had undertaken in 1963 and, as a text, was not completed until 44 years later with the 2007 publication of *The Complete Poetry of César Vallejo.* As a figure of resistance to be assimilated, Vallejo has become, over the long haul, a crucial aspect of whatever skill I have managed as a poet, as well as the primary gift that has enabled me to exercise my faculties at large as a writer and translator. By calling him a Spectre, I seek to emphasize his interior, against-the-grain combustion that has increased my courage to immerse myself in that negation necessary to test whatever affirmation my work has been able to proclaim.

## In Memory of George Butterick

For a tribute to this poet and Charles Olson scholar, see Paul Christensen's essay "The Achievement of George Butterick" in *Sulfur* 21, 1988. The ten issues of the magazine *OLSON: Journal of the Charles Olson Archive* (1974–1977) that Butterick edited are essential for any thorough engagement with Olson's writings. Butterick's poems are collected in *The Collected Poems of George Butterick*, The Poetry / Rare Books Collection, SUNY at Buffalo, Buffalo, N.Y., 1988.

## Poem Beginning with a Question
## from Charles Simic's Review of Louise Gluck's *Averno*

Simic's review appeared in the July 22, 2006 issue of *The New York Review of Books*.

## Octavio's Labyrinth

About one-third of the lines in this poem are from Eliot Weinberger's excellent translations of Octavio Paz's poetry in *The Collected Poems of Octavio Paz*, New Directions, N.Y.C., 1987.

## The Left Foot of King Ramesses I

Information on tent caterpillars comes from *The Tent Caterpillars* by Terrence D. Fitzgerald, Comstock Publishing Associates, Ithaca N.Y., 1995.

## Matterhorn, Western Face

A large portion of the photograph addressed in this poem may be found on the cover of *Bradford Washburn / Mountain Photography*, ed. Anthony Decaneas, The Mountaineers, 1999.

The first ascent of this mountain took place in 1865. A party made up of Edward Whymper, Charles Hudson, Lord Francis Douglas, Douglas Robert Hadow, Michel Croz, and the two Peter Taugwalders (father and son) reached the summit via the Hömli Ridge in Switzerland. While descending, Hadow, Croz, Hudson and Douglas fell to their deaths on the Matterhorn Glacier and all but Douglas (whose body was never found) are buried in the Zermatt churchyard.

For commentary on "the hole that became a pole" see pp. 232–236 of *Juniper Fuse: Upper Paleolithic Imagination & the Construction of the Underworld*, Wesleyan University Press, second edition, 2008.

### Reading Laura Solórzano

This poem was generated out of several enthusiastic bilingual readings of Solórzano's *Lip Wolf*, Action Books, Notre Dame, IN., 2007, accurately and imaginatively translated by Jen Hofer. The Pale Man scene from the film *Pan's Labyrinth* makes a brief appearance here.

### Poem to Help Will Alexander Fight Cancer

This poem was written to be read at a benefit poetry reading for Will Alexander, that I helped organize, at Skylight Books in Los Angeles, on January 13, 2008.

### Black Paradise

This poem is in part a response to my reading Stephen Barber's book, *Terminal Curses*, Solar Books, 2008, which addresses the 406 notebooks that Antonin Artaud kept from 1945 to the last night of his life, March 3/4, 1948. Barber is the leading English-language authority on Artaud's work, and also the author of *Antonin Artaud / Blows and Bombs*, Faber and Faber, London, 1993; *Weapons of Liberation*, Faber and Faber, 1996; and *The Screaming Body*, Creation Books, 1999.

For material on Sedna, see *Juniper Fuse: Upper Paleolithic Imagination & the Construction of the Underworld*, p. 277.

The Cosquer cave is a few miles south of Marseilles (where Artaud was born in 1896). It is reached by a shaft 120 feet below the water surface which leads to a large chamber 490 feet beyond the shaft's entrance. 20,000 years ago the shore line was roughly 360 feet away from the Cosquer's entrance. When the ice melted, and the water rose, it filled the lower parts of the cave, sealing off the rest. Cosquer is the only Upper Paleolithic painted cave with sea animals. Besides horses, ibex, chamois, bovids and cervids, there are 8 seals, 3 great auks, a fish, and several jellyfish. For an overview of Cosquer, see *The Cave Beneath the Sea*, Abrams, N.Y.C., 1996, by Jean Clottes and Jean Courtin.

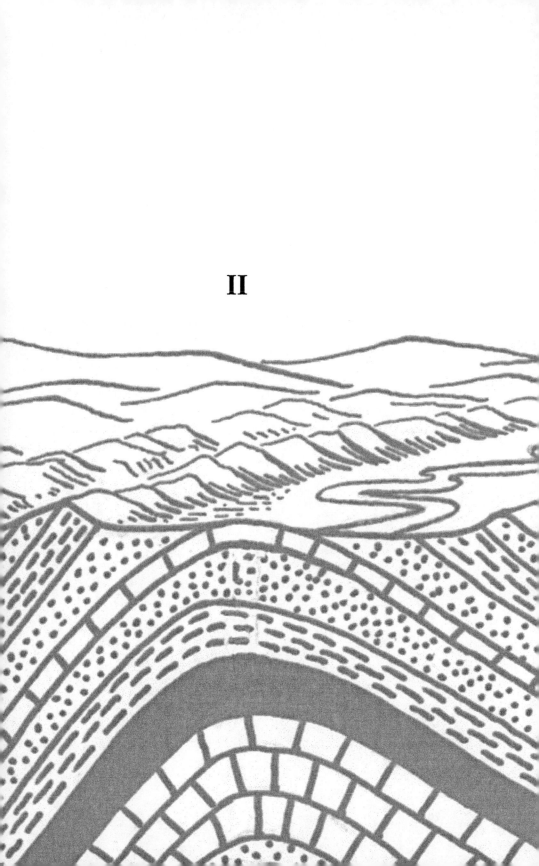

**II**

# TAVERN OF THE SCARLET BAGPIPE

## Introduction

In 1979 I visited the Prado Museum in Madrid and spent half an hour before Hieronymus Bosch's *Garden of Earthly Delights*. For the past fifteen years, I have had framed reproductions of that painting and the Lisbon *Temptation of Saint Anthony* on my workroom wall. I have found both of these triptychs impossible to take in while looking at them on the wall. They have hung there, steely challenges, over the years. I have collected books and articles on Bosch, waiting for the right moment to engage at least one of these masterpieces.

In 2003 I proposed a one-month "Bosch project" for a residency at the Rockefeller Study Center at Bellagio on Lake Como in Italy. My idea was to spend two months going through my materials and then, while at the Study Center, write into *The Garden of Earthly Delights*. My residency was accepted in May 2004, and my wife Caryl and I left for the Center on October 18.

I took along with me a rolled-up reproduction of the triptych in a tube, a xerox of Wilhelm Fraenger's chapter "The Millennium: Outlines of an Interpretation" from his book, *Bosch*, a copy of Laurinda Dixon's *Alchemical Imagery in Bosch's Garden of Earthly Delights*, a xerox of Michel de Certeau's "The Garden: Delirium and Delights of Hieronymus Bosch" (from his *The Mystic Fable*, a book I discovered while reading Robin Blaser's poem, "Image-Nation 25, Exody"), a couple of pages of bird lists from Terry Tempest Williams' *Leap*, and John Rowland's *The Garden of Earthly Delights / Hieronymus Bosch*, which reproduces colored panels of the triptych in the original size. Being able to study separate portions in detail partially solved the problem of how to identify everything.

Once at the Center, I tacked the reproduction (about one-third the size of the nine by seven foot original) to large sheets of cardboard and leaned it against the wall on a table next to my desk. In front of me was a window vista of a pristine cloud, mountain, lake scape, where the Como and Lecco lakes joined. The same vista, I felt, could have been beheld in the 19th century. It would not have been strange to have seen Shelley or Rilke strolling through the olive grove a hundred feet below and beyond my window.

I re-read my materials for a week, then continued to re-read while studying the reproduction, checking details in the Rowland edition, and writing notes in a large notebook. While I sometimes disagreed with Fraenger and Dixon (both, in my view, impose elaborate systems on the triptych, moving it into a rational perspective rather than acknowledging its many obscurities), both writers had really studied Bosch's painting, as had de Certeau, and their detailed commentaries helped me notice the "minute particulars" that proliferate throughout it. After two weeks, I hit the Bosch "wall" that I imagine all serious viewers of *The Garden of Earthly Delights* experience: there is no core meaning to uncover. Certain figures and image-combines appear to be the fruits of Bosch's inventive arsenal and there is nothing at hand to call them. As someone attempting to write into the painting, I found myself in the position expressed by a line in a poem by Michel Deguy: "I know, or I invent."

Three areas in the "Eden" and "Paradise" panels offered very substantial challenges: the constructions along the top of these panels which I ended up calling The Terrestrial Transformers, and, in the lower part of the "Paradise" panel, the static melée of nudes and fruit. While at the Study Center I spent a week carefully describing what I saw in these areas. When I began to work on the poem itself, back in Ypsilanti, I realized that pages of detailed description were going to stop my work in its tracks. I ended up with a brief poem identifying the "Eden" Transformers which suggests what their role in the unfolding of the triptych might be, along with an appendix which reflects on their weird, unique forms in both panels. For a section of the poem on the frieze of nudes, I borrowed some phrases from Frank O'Hara's poem, "In Memory of my Feelings," a fantasia on his various selves. Given the similarity of nearly all the nudes, I conceived them as a multitude of the doubles of a single, roving persona.

As always in the past, Caryl helped me a lot with my project. At the Study Center, she went online for information about the mysterious red fruitballs and put me in contact with Dale Pendell, whose letter in response to my query I decided to include in one of the appendices. Back in Ypsilanti, she went through my one hundred pages of notes with me, and helped me to understand that the process of studying and attempting to assimilate the painting, while significant, was less crucial to display than a poem in which all my research was reorganized into an imaginative structure.

CHARCOAL CURDLING CLOUDS.         [*The Third Day of Creation.*
Scallops of light weakly illuminating earth's flat disk.     The Closed Wings.
Desire swarming in its orbicular bath.                 Genesis]

Arching out of an egg-like container, a sprout drooping
a fruitball.
                Muggy haze. Larval moil.
Clumps of trees with ghost-porous fruit.
Three timid pink lights on a peaked "mushroom"
                  resting on a "millstone."

"Firecracker" with a long "fuse."
Thorned rinds. Shells of earth ovens-to-come.
The distillation that reigns in my body and soul
              11 A.M. October 26, 2004.
           Window over Lake Como,    blue-gray
furry mist, headlands no more substantive than clouds.

Pronged fragments. Blasted "pear."
Scintillae in slug-like blue swellings.

           Genesis 3rd day water
gauze-opaque with the nearly-existent.

FOUR TERRESTRIAL TRANSFORMERS

swept, clustered, by swifts.

The first:

an apricot, mosque-like, spindle-shaped tower.
A large cored ball, below which
a disk turns into a dark brown Jehovah (or Moses?)
on his back, arm raised, tablet
   resting on his chest...

The second:

squat, cleft "female" husk, dark blue with
"amanita" white dots. A prehistoric maw fixed
open. Tiny pink owl perched on
the tip of the lower jaw...

The third:

rounded blue mound in mineral cloak. Genesis
3rd day jagged "male" pinnacle with sprout drooping
   a blue-speared pod...

The fourth:

two vertical millstones linked by a curving leafless branch
arcing over white fruit-clustered bushy trees
   set between the stones...

Monuments to the 3rd day of Creation.

Four organless hosts. Commandment remains.

MONKEY CROUCHED ON A WHITE ELEPHANT. [Eden.
Albino giraffe. Two-legged dogalope. Left Wing. Middle &
On hind legs a lizard cavorting before a surly boar Lower Sections.]
   accompanied by five babies.
Carnivore ripping a supine deer's belly.
Creator. Just-awakened Adam. Downward-gazing Eve.


There's a hybrid evolutionary nuance at the edge of the pond
spontaneously generating creatures.
Three-headed phoenix yapping at a spoonbill.
Small sea horse with platework mane.


               Floating,
the God-author has reappeared with his book
as a dolphin-duck-monk or a platypus-seal. He might even be
a sea monk "known for luring people near the water,
then eating them." *What is in this creature's book?*
Overhearing me, an owl lowers its eyes to
dark blue rubble glinting with test tubes, red berries
on which rests    the Fountain of Life.


Red, white Tantrik ingredients blend in the Creator's pink robe,
glow in his flesh. In contrast:
ivory-white Eve, bemused Adam.
The Biblical rib
earlier a bone lady, who must trace back to Ice Age statuettes.
I wonder:
          might this Fountain of Life—
a mineral-plant-monstrance,
liquids peeing through orbs and disks,
balanced on percolating muck
—be the pumping heartwork of an androgynous matrix?


The "gears" appear to be interior orb struts,
eyeball homunculi, or puppet-
pupils, globes and berries, red fruitballs, pearls.


The Tree of Life (*Dracaena draco*)
exudes red sap ("prized for improving strength and for staunching
   the flow of blood").

Its fleshy tripartite limbs are hung with large gold discs
interspersed with black, red, white tendrilled fruit clusters.
Swollen branches create a saurian presence.

A murder of crows hesitates,
before hustling into the hole in a big egg.

The Tree of Knowledge is a Phoenix Palm
coiled by a humble black snake.
Black frogs, black three-headed salamanders, creatures
popping out of creatures, scuttle up onto a clay embankment
shaped like young Salvador Dali's head in profile,
his "eye" a centipede with spiky feelers, bird-droopy tail,
    wearing a silver mussel timepiece.

               Good morning, Salvador!
Hieronymus has given you a crested black snake moustache.
Your timepiece eye makes you appear asleep.
Best that you are, or you'd freak out over the slime-black
traffic probing where your neck might be. Something black, long-tailed,
has already burrowed into the base of your skull.

               Dali invented by Bosch!
Dali as a Bosch cyborg clanking down 5th Avenue in the NYC 1960s,
unaware that the semen reservoir in his skull was populated by Bosch
             beetles in Dodgem bang!

BOSCH'S EDEN POOL OF SPONTANEOUS GENERATION    [*Eden.*
is a kind of Cenoté with scarlet-rust cisternal limestone walls.    Left Wing.
A pheasant exposes her anus as she sticks her head into the    Lower
   pool's cypress-black sheen.    Section.]
A male pheasant stares at the female's anus.
A stump-legged otter drags its fish-end up on the bank.
A black crayfish-headed bird prepares to spit a supine black frog on its
   scissor-beak (while a shore bird with skeletal peacock tail prepares
   to gut the frog).
A cat walks away from the pool, eyes glazed, mouse nape in teeth.
A clack-billed ghoul-bird grips twitching frog legs between its fever-
   beaded "lips."

The pool tunnels out of Eden and leads to pools in Paradise, Apocalypse:
   these are the subterranean waterworks of the triptych.

THE HAY-COLORED GRASS OF PARADISE HAS THIGH SHAPES,
one angling off toward Eden, the other toward Apocalypse.     [*Paradise.*
They evoke legs of a sacrificed goddess body               Central Panel.
whose mons veneris contains a circular pool.               Middle Section.]

Thirty-one female nudes cavort in mother-elixir.
Ravens, storks flit, rest on their heads.
Transformation of the Cenoté.
They are wooed by a rotating cavalcade:

little red bear under a horse. Bud-like clusters of mainly nude male riders,
   all identical.
A crow sits on a long thin branch piercing huge grapes.
Circling cocks, camels, prancing ponies.
Black-winged stilt poking its needle-beak into the anus of an upturned
   leg-forked lad.
Chatting youths, wearing tern, woodpecker headdresses.
On a large white boar, one holds up and spreads a heron's wings.
Transformation of the millstone. Labor converted to a snorting, heaving
   bend-about.
Bull, donkey. Pronghorn with Hathor fruit sun between horns.
Leaping, static, this engine of the mind.
About what hub does the creative wind?
                         A nymph-clustered pool?
Three riders bear a fish devouring another fish (one pats the devourer
   as if it were a pet).
Lateral entry: an immense lobster shell packed with dirty asses
   plugging its orifice, carried by a platoon of nudes—
drive this too into the carousel! Griffon with jet-black-tipped wings,
   round porcupine blazon.
Lion lugging a huge carp. Two storks on the back of a rose boar
   with black balls, a black-and-white-suckered-tentacle-tail.
Lavender leopard with goggle-black eyes. All are astrologically-
   tinged, medicinal, layered with superstitial abuse.

Another lateral entry (the strangest "creature construction" in the trip-
tych): to the cavalcade's left, male nudes, packed in a circle, some up-
right, others standing on their heads, serve as the pedestal of a dark-blue
pod holding a dull pink scarlet-dotted fruit topped by a marabou head. A
fat black rat is making its way down the marabou's beak, the far end of

which (no longer a beak but an antenna) is being tugged forward by a male attempting to pull this whole "thing" into the cavalcade. Topping the marabou's head is a red pod out of which a pair of legs stick straight up. Out of the pod's bottom, an arm reaches down around the marabou head. On this pod's far side, a sketchy figure seems to be trying to pull if off. Jutting out of the dark-blue pod are enormous hornbill legs and talons. Perched on the right talon: is it a brown insect or a bird-shaped turd?

SO FROM ONE PERSPECTIVE, GOD THE FATHER, [The entire
placed by Bosch in a lunar vault, brings into view, triptych]
then conducts, this terrestrial symphony,
reproducing himself as the Son, or a Creator Christ,
   who then molds Adam.
That's a lot of guydom, clearly shamanic; apprentices
reproducing magic selves via obscure masters or ur-generators.

Might not the swarm of "human" wraiths percolating Paradise
be the progeny of an exfoliating vision by which "holy ghosts"
are brought into a physical conversation-
conversion with birds, beasts, flowers, fruit?

This grand array of nudes does not include copulation—
or none that I can see. If I can't see it,
Bosch is making a point by leaving it out.
There are many penises, all are flaccid, there's no pubic hair,
suggesting adults with a pre-pubescent sexuality.
The women also lack pubic hair and have small breasts.

The gold coins on the Eden Tree of Life
reappear only in Apocalypse, where a crouched man
shits four of them into a caricature of the Cenoté.

(Nearby, a Vanitas scene: the face of a collapsed maiden—felt up by a
large dark mouse with salamander-feet hands—is distorted in an anal
mirror—with jagged metallic rim evoking a chastity belt—attached to
the butt of a green demon whose legs are forked hazel tree branches).

Hence, in Bosch, Apocalypse is "coined" in Eden.

*It is not a breakdown brought about by paradisal transgression.*

So here I am, up in the sky riding a griffin with Persian-blue aquiline
      wings,
holding a branch from the Tree of Life upon which a red starling
      perches.
In its talons my griffin grips a wriggling bear.
As a unit, we herald the commingling of all things,
or as many as one artist can atoll, in the coral amassment of a life.

I look down on mer-knight occupied lakes, flesh forts trembling in the
folds of lightning-spiked sleep.

In Bosch's era, the subconscious was more altar-definite than today,
architecture more magical.
There is a translucent, glazed, interpenetrating liquidity here,
an image rhythm between Paradise and the foundations of being.
Orbital, iridescent variations are repeated with reassuring familiarity.
There is hardly a thorn that does not express its bulb, as if apocatastasis
were the underlying magnetism.
And yet, near the peak of the fourth Transformer, a ripped-out elephant
tusk hammers home: "If it is marvelous, kill it," linking that world to
ours.

I am also a mer-knight on a flying fish, pulling my tail up over my head,
a salamander pout on my armored mug.

I give a functionality to the void, instilling it with a gear-work of
irrational transmission.

Each gap is populated by a great fretted clarinet farting black swifts, or
by the adoration of a giant strawberry.

Madness to be here, so let's slip back into the egg, or feed a cherry the
size of our heads to a blood-red dolphin.

Did the New World dream its way into Bosch in 1500?

In a barge with a half-moon prow, a white maiden stiffens as a black
male climbs onto her.

Two nudes in touching headstands, called a "Pythagorean candle," on
the equatorial shelf banding the Life Globe.

Better to drag a big speckled bug around by the tail than seek
redemption.

Is not the omnipresence of birds a sign that everything is about to
re-hatch?

to be born and to live as variously as possible."
Eider Duck. Hoopoe. Robin. Goldfinch.
Kingfisher. Mallard. Displays more gorgeous than humankind.
Goldfinch offers grapes to three of me.
My eyes beseech you, dear other, as I advance on the maiden of myself,
    trapped in a floating pod.
On my Green Woodpecker mount I wear a flask helmet.
I am Iranian when I embrace Tawny Owl.

Translucent globe in which I sit, caressing my sister self.
Retort warmed by the urgent, passionate heart of a thistle.
"They look like gods, these white men."
Upside down in the pool, my hands flop to cover my balls.
Out of the red pod caught between my thrust-up thighs:
    an adult heron, a shrike.

"My body, the naked host to my many selves."
How beautiful to offer an eighty-pound blackberry to eleven former
    selves.
This sister-white brother-red berry is expressing its Orphic
    immortality—will it ever peacock out?

"What land is this, so free?"
To live in a tentacular burr whose thistle flower feeds an aglossa moth.
To rise into the cool noon sky on a winged fish.
Will this speared fruitball rudder direct me? How flex my dolphin
    hybridity?

Always my coral-red tent and the dynamite berries offered by cousin Jay.
Always the leg-entwined mirth as eight of me tilt our heads back,
    famished for—what *is* this fruit?
How account for its landscape-altering chimes?

"The scene of my selves, the occasion of these ruses"
Sturgeon under arm, I see it is time to abandon the belvedere where I
    completed my novitiate.
From Strawberry Bonnet Lookout, three of me watch three of us
    "watch the ripple of our loss disappear."

Is not part of the magic of multifoliate being to co-exist with vacuums
   and dead ends?

"The heart bubbles with red ghosts, since to move is to love."
Under transparent bindweed, I take the veil.
Squeezing me like an orange for some sign of vitality
the sky breaks out in freckled baby-apple white!

                                   O I too am Adam,
a funhouse with a thousand mirrors, each undulant with nude wraiths.
Combing each mirror to conjure Eve, I exchange heads with Horned
   Owl.
I milk flowers like poisonous snakes. My breath
   is the gross form of time.
                         "Dance the orange?" I dance
the spheres of origin, oyster-potent, exuding instead of semen, pearls!

               A unicorn breaks free.
I saddle him with the multifaceted insight of a fly.
"How do you know," he asks, "that all your selves are not really just one
   projected as many in a fly's eye?"

                              That calls for some champagne
from a pear the size of a pig! A liquid of pure obstruction!
So do I course my spine in reverse Kundalini,
opening vein pubs,
tying off sorrow restrictions,
immortality morbidity, God,
and with Him, all scriptures listing demarcations.

"But who will stay to be these numbers when all the lights are dead?"
Inside this hollowed-out pumpkin, there is nightshade for my souls.
For my sister hermit crabs this Olmec cranium will become a lodge.

I dial the mystic pudenda in the globe-hole of the Fountain of Life.

The gigantomachy in my mind blows off black milk.

Varnishing the green with a weedy screech: the idiot flute player
   at the center of creation.

WINE-SHAFTED LIGHT BOILING WITH ASHEN SPRAY.   [*Apocalypse.*
Horned men with pikes scuttling between gutted towers.        Right Wing.
Fuscohyaline clouds coiling neverward. Ember-prancing blasts      Upper &
fed with fleecy scorch. The sky grays as if ocean dry         Middle Sections.]
were tidal-waving through. Fire like raw running amber wounds.
                                        Dun-black sky
by falling, arching bodies pricked. Wastes in the night sky,
    wastes merged with mountain char.


Below in the scalding lake, specks of the drowning like streaks of mold.
Pouring across a bridge's molten slash, an army led by
a salamander-saddled ghoul. Windmill slats glazed with flame.
Out of the roily blood-colored bay writhing naked clumps
    wave, sink back…


        Light blasts through a prison gate
illuminating a chalk-white tree. A possum-tailed warrior
climbs a ladder lit by curlicues of cinder-red fire
swooshing across twig-folk, insectile wisps.


                Come closer: spoonbilled ghosts
with longbows mix with masked cacodemons. Gigantic ears
like bloated gonads hug each side of an Omega blade.
                            A hooded churl
tries to wrest a dying nude up into an earlobe pouch.


Does any landscape remain? Or is there only shifting murk
    disemboweling into a grand putrification?


Below an enormous cow skull, a human-clappered bell-rope
pulled by a fat bogle raging with glee,
                his tail coiling down
                like a speckled
                eel of shit.


A lout, shouldering a hockey stick, an arrow sticking out his ass,
climbs up a ladder, past an ashen tree arm stuffed
in a rowboat. Another arm of white petrified bark, its branch piercing
an egg-shell thorax, rises from a second foundered boat.

Attached to the branch: a white flag with a scarlet bagpipe:
>    *Tavern of the Scarlet Bagpipe,*
rinsed fire-red inside. A soul and his mates sit transfixed by one
  whose whole head is a blood soak.

The Tavern's human head, in front of its thorax shell,
turns to look back, perhaps Bosch himself.
Long straggly ash-blond hair, mouth at once smile and sneer,
the right eye trance-intense, staring back across
the hump of his tree "shoulder" at something off-canvas.
Is Apocalypse to be fixed open to the world,
to be a tree house saloon into which any guzzler can climb?
Artist as tavern aslosh with the lightning of Dionysian over-reach,
  pickled melancholy...
>    For a hat the Tavern head wears a white disk
>    crowned by a self-propelled bagpipe
around which there's a rotary parade...

A white-capped clawed hag points the chanter,
the reed pipe fumes at the weird folk trundling the disk.
Circular emanations: berries, pools, roundness repeated to the point
  all seems in thrall to cogs...

—just now I spotted a dotted-white red bug-like creature.
>    Is *Amanita muscaria* involved?

This flash-frozen nightmare.  It is the onlooker
who puts motion into Apocalypse. Expressionless male faces, dots
  or blotches where eyes should be. Who are they? Who am I?
This vision is a kind of mirror facing me, likewise a mirror.
>              Between our banks
  a drama surges, ripe with circular cease and wheel.

IN THE ISSENHEIM ALTARPIECE, FEATHER-ADORNED ANGELS
play gorgeous instruments. The loin-cloth of Christ,         *[Apocalypse.*
whose spiked hands shriek, is classy too.         Right Wing.
Bosch's handsome lute-harp, hurdy-gurdy, bombardon—why     Lower
    are they in Apocalypse?         Section.]
To sing it in? Embed it in onlooker conscience?
Gangs of gape-skewed singers, mixed in with fiends.
Out of the fish-mouth of one towel-headed ghoul a beaded saliva-line
arches toward the musically-notated ass of another
   crushed by the lute-harp.

BABOOM of the bombardon, played like a bazooka.
A concert for Saturn Nighthawk, or "the goatsucker kid," in high chair
   potty,
                  with a diaper winding sheet,
cramming a bird-farting body into his opened shredder beak,
                      a cocked cauldron for a crown,
death-blue body, polioed legs stuffed into potty-attached jugs.
Translucent blue intestines balloon down from the potty hole,
   releasing two souls into the cess.

Is Saturn Nighthawk "eating his children" the chick from the broken-
shelled Tavern? Parody of The Father in his lunar Genesis vault
and the Creator Son, in pink, cathecting Eve and Adam?

My favorite ghoul is holding high a gaming board,
pot-belly filled with pus and fire, and is he happy!
Every gambler groan makes him cum. A bunch of grapes
corks his navel a second before its hydrant spurt.
He's got a disk on his head to mock the Fountains and pools
—why it's his Easter Bonnet! Raise high the roof beams of soul
ruined in gambling's lethal ennui. His chum is sticking a knife into
the guts of some expressionless guy who he's also choking.
White mouse head, ermine cloak, squat chubby black legs in clogs:
a really fashionable fuck! To his back is attached a tray-like disk,
with die and lopped-off hand by kitchen knife impaled. Specter of the
   trinity
haunting all things, this triptych as a triskelion bandsaw.

An armored Fido snacks on master throat. He's got his own doggy steel-
spiked disk-hat.

A gryllos has hopped forth. He wants at that naked nabob being felt up
by a sow Mother Superior to sign a new deed. More property for the
    church!
And this gryllos is a real sweetheart: fat shit-stained lizard legs,
a maw of helmet-work from which hangs a chopped-off foot.
                            From his long lower beak an ink well swings.
The sow Superior has a quill. But it's all a nightmare, no? So why not
    sign?

Squire Rabbit has arrived with hunting horn, game bag, and naked slut
whose belly is farting fire. She's hung by her heels from his pike—
so, the hunting's been good! So good the butchered creatures
    have turned the tables.
Think of the earth from a rabbit hutch point of view. Can you imagine
the cow report if slaughterhouse reality could be mooed?
Or the hook-torn trout assembly granted a symposium of the creek?
    Apocalypse is what *we* have done to *them.*

LOVERS INSIDE A MUSSEL SHELL EXCRETING PEARLS.          [The
Like hermit crabs, these nudes: any interior is home.          entire triptych.
The great regression to the primordial athanor,          —and beyond]
the mother sea slurp and bubble of watery dark where dreaming is so
    intense it is a whirring honeycomb.

In these improvisations off the force of Bosch
male squadrons shovel coal into a pulsing white queen who births
    upon ignition.
A Zoa-ball in which fetuses are singing like canaries in their skeletal
    cradles.
Discombobulated rug-cutters, crowns askew, blast apart as the fetuses
    turn into Katzenjammer imps.
                              The vision whips back into Eden:
in his vulvar side, Adam is a smoking retort of androgynous spleen.
Bumblebee kings are crouching and cooing about the manger barge:
"Just who is this Holy Ghost who impregnates from afar?"
                              Aztec culture zips in:
a ball of feathers drops on Coatlicue out sweeping—voilá!
She's pregnant with Huitzilopochtli. Out squirms the king of war.

Just what is in that black testicular pod from which we've been drinking?
Not the keelson of creation Walt Whitman called love!
Fools have been let onto our Ship of Death, a sarcophagus is its keel.
Do we dare take on our own impassioned reality?
Can we tack into the spills of infant terror mistranslated and stored?
For all artists are naked facing the ladder pointing toward this Tavern.
Yet no single imagination can perform apocatastasis.
Wholeness is uterine, all roads are scabs over the wounds of diaspora.

Hear yourself whinny as you strain to toss a fruitball
    to a dolphin performing for her supper.
The crowd roars. The fire in the circus will never be put out—
flames will destroy the giant mallards, the half-submerged earless owl,
but the crowd will continue to demand more victims for the solar maw,
as if life to continue requires Aztec carnage.

The intoxications of immortality light up the switchboards when
    someone is murdered.

The furnaces of immortality are fed with the bodies of people who look
    a little different than us.
How does this work, Donald Rumsfeld?
Does your Reaper retreat an inch for each sixteen-year-old Iraqi boy
    snipered while out looking for food?
Men with political power are living pyramids of slaughtered others.
Bush is a Babelesque pyramid of blood-scummed steps.
The discrepancy
between the literal suit and psychic veracity is nasty to contemplate.
Imagine a flea with a howitzer shadow
or a worm whose shade is a nuclear blaze.

BOSCH BROKE HIMSELF, AN EGG, INTO AN ABYSS     [*Apocalypse.
where yolk and white weaved themselves into tapestries     Right Wing.
  roaring with world-end winds.     Middle Section.]
Each fiber an incomplete soul, a tapeworm wriggling for jointure.
Are all endings the failure to connect with source?
Thread thoughts. Fictives, one by one,
wiggle out of the Cenoté in honor of Herr Otter
bringing Cro-Magnon ore up out of the myth-obscure creature dream.
Merely to be. As a salp. Merely to be. Even as a sun ray.


"You need two beached rowboats for a real Ship of Fools,"
Hieronymus finally spoke, "one for each of my blasted trees.
I rest on what is left of Life and Knowledge.
The scene in the Tavern is shabby, true,
an old alchemical hangover, no lead into gold, rather:
melancholy into war, the Philosopher Stone endlessly
mistranslated as personal immortality…
I love my Paradise of alchemical foreplay,
but then libido shifts into a sanguine gear…
volcanoes discover their sperm, maidens rebuild themselves
  to bear children, creatures
become fixed in size. What's going on?
Life overwhelming imagination! And desire?
Locked into artifact, its tumblers spin, a catastrophe zodiacal
in its invasion of the orbicular, reducing miracles to
  salvation, dragging in the lemur dark…"


Standing on the Tavern's ladder I heard but could not see Hieronymus.
He seemed to speak as one staring at the impossibility of
  the fulfillment of desire,
hoarse, bemused, fascinated perhaps, that I'd made it this far.
I watched the pink bagpipe bulge and honk at the circling
Adamites gripped by morphine dreams.
The bagpipe kept flashing reintegration in the cenoté of my mind.
Hmm… Adam and Eve do not produce children,
they produce doubles. Fairy-blooded berries.
No children. Menstrual ingots. Red ochre from the cosmic dive,
mind capsized into the body's basins.
Loss we float in. Sunset porridge. Vaginal aurora.
The sputtering flames of sulfuric recollections.

I reached the opening, peered into the Tavern.
Old woman in fool's cap, forked, as if by snail horns,
   kneeling by a cask, drawing wine.
Three Adamites, skin frosty scarlet, reared back in trance.
A long vermilion table over which a black-eyed chick dissolved in flame.
One had for a chair a black semi-squashed amphibian.
Beside them, the head of a huge white blood-snouted boar.
   Again, Hieronymus:
      "In s'Hertogenbosch, I envisioned the layers
of all these studies. Out of what you call my Cenoté
arose creatures never known or named.
They generated a roving curtain of rain, lightning-lit, thunder-rotten,
the never-seen-before revising the taxonomy of experience.
These curtains parted to reveal an age outside ambivalence:
nudes in self-propagating, accidental combines,
tendrilous stately phantoms in discordant strews,
as if they'd just tumbled, dazed, out of the Tree of Life.
I caught some in the basket of this panel, in a grand seeming-to-be...
However, man is a mask-canopied thatch of beings.
Look at that plum-headed seductioner,
stretched out on lawn pad, ear-tongueing a captivated lass.
There is an abyss between intention and reception.
Do the seductioner's words become builders in her?
Do these innocent masons begin to raise walls?
Do these walls become a church? And one with thumb-screws?
Who is responsible for the apocalyptic penetration of Eden?
Who"—and here he faltered—"is responsible for the way
   a tale's meaning is construed?
The human mind is a maze with holes and crushers.
Who knows into what     this ball of a tale will roll?"


            Then the hag mumbled:
"And the ferrets in my womb would starve
were it not for the compote of armor and tripe to be found in
   the goal of masculinity.
Ah! Invasion is the sweetest tomb!
You who have turned against war must project your trolls
if you do not want your mother's soul to be hanged,
a plumb line, between experience and vision."

Voices to trust? Or mischievous ghosts?
Psychic instruction moves like Shiva through an underworld
    deck of fables, shuffle-dancing them
so that the quester can hardly tell rung from Rapunzel.
Where psyche is followed, the world folds with every word,
    a cinnamon tease
swift as a towering vertigo. The subconscious taps a madder light,
vibrating wizard-cruciform insight, innocent, venomous.
Composed of water and slime the stream of the imaginal
    circles and binds.
Each present enfolds its own Alpha and Omega,
each action an obligation, a bond, enchased
in whatever fortitude I've inherited from Okeanos.

TO MARRY A MARLIN
while mounted on a paw-lifted feline.
This panopticonic
blackberry
floats. Our faces, its halo.
Orange moth feeding in blue thistle light.
Passed out, at noon. Take his pulse
as our Master took Eve's.
V for Vanitas, legs forked, head submerged.
Pearls as a pod's ejaculate.
Strawberry knapsack with blue
petal plastered to ass.
Mouth open for a cherry
proffered by eider duck bill.
Amused at her hesitation to taste
her own brain. Or is that just a septic berry?
To read by sphincter light.
Haddock body full of roe.
Patting it from the inside of a trefoiled urn.
Sinking his teeth into a cushion-sized
plum. Trying to divine
the spilled pearls' I Ching
fate glyph. Paradise
on the verge of an Apocalyptic break-
down. Big mouse
freaked out in glass tube by fruit-
enchanted human face.
Male forms as feelers.
Nude maiden covered with trans-
lucent hair. Petunia hair clip.
Put clothes on one of them, blend his garb
with cavern blackness. Let him plumb
the new Eve, lips
under seal. Clasp
the floating owl. Does it know
my hand on its feathered breast?
Am *I* swearing upon
*it?* Headstand in fish-flower tights.
Everything
part of a filamentous

[The entire
triptych.]

structure.
Do I know this race? Have they ever
existed? Balancing
the eider duck on my upraised calves.
Rumps showing through
mussel shell crack—lugged by their son?
Less strange than a finch
offering grapes to a straining
ashen bather. Four-
legged jig. Fruit rattles. Shiva-
armed. Owl stoned on
OM. Soul apples for the picking.
Offering the crow perched on
my upturned foot
the Eden apple's worm.
Look how tenderly, transported
by mallard, I touch
her Ethiopian neck.
The kingfisher's
red claws. Entangled in hoopoe crest.
Basking in a hoop: bright-red caterpillar.
Tendril intensity:
the signature of all probes.
Rotary mermaid tail.
Glob
out of which Jesus might have stepped.
Luscious berries shining in muck,
rot azure. Steaming
Eden swamp. Egg-shaped
reptile. Marble-still Adam.
Amazed to be the fire in a mermaid's tail
roasting her under-fin.
Ground breaking out in white
berry rash. Under skin sensation of
slithering silver fish.
Is this mushroom or aphid mind?
Chugalugging the black pod's
groin mash. Mead
as the honeyed air. Strawberry
burden too sweet to bear. So,

doze,
perched in shrub-crotch.
The new Eve
spotted through a chakra-
embossed glass pillar.
Vermilion hand of the master
checking old Eve's pulse.
Divinity
as hair cascade, golden
tress drop, blonde cobra hood
curtaining her ass. Ghost
owl in the peaks of Eden.
Metaphysical ba-
zooka belching swifts.
Circular raven with pendulum-whip
tail. A strawberry crown
for the naked male-molded pudding.
Tush
sporting a nose-gay.
Dance the horned owl. Sepal-headed
cowboy on static
pecker. Birds as the royal
appointments in Paradise. Where
are the fathers? Under knight armor?
And the mothers—wearing fool's caps?
Third Movement of The Apocatastatic Rumba.
Kingdom
built on jig-sawed
foreplay. The Child at five as Saturn
Nighthawk
munching on a father bar.
Anality
as Vanitas with hazel knees.
Behold: Saturn Nighthawk has shat
his adolescence-to-be
through the blue
infancy bulb and has entered
the pool system!
He kicks through sewage, makes
the long swim back through

the Paradise pool of waiting maidens,
to reach
the Cenoté ooze of Eden, finally
to surface as our hybrid author.
Maybe
in the nautical platypus's
blank book
he will pen some words of
Genesis
restitution, some frog-leg wriggling lingo.

FOLD THE EDEN PANEL TO THE RIGHT,       *[Third Day of Creation.*
the Apocalypse panel to the left. Now, nearly touching,   The Closed Wings.
they are no longer separated by Paradise.          Ablution.]*

These panels are the Lady of Eden, the Lord of Apocalypse.

Together at last, face down, side by side,
the beginning and the end, they stare into fulfillment,
integrating themselves into Paradise,
injecting realization with innocence and experience,
creating that realm we call the subconscious:
Road of Awe, without antithesis.
Destruction is affirmation is creation.

Theseus copulates with, while slaughtering, the Minotaur.
The logic of metaphor weds the logic of biology.
Man and beast, spider-to-spider, in the web gum of the soul.

The backs of Eden and Apocalypse show what
  earth     was
on the cusp of life.
They instill us with this genesis
when a planet spun from dust, rock, carbon
compounds and silicon, out-gassed water and spliced
carbon-bearing molecules,
                      a kind of auto-
constructing Meccano of inconceivable complexity:

primitive tissue, the spiral structure of nucleic acids,
phosphorus, clays, RNA,
                  tiny bubbles known as lipid vesicles,
a simulacrum, a marionette without strings—
                  bacterial
hyperthermophiles, Hadic creatures
happy in hot vats that torture
all other life, to dine upon sulfur,
the branching tree of descent,
          early cells tacky with mucus,

pyritiferous seep, black smokers, photosynthesis
and the creation of oxygen
                    —stromatolithic altar!

End-censed renewal of Genesis!
As if a thousand-year rain had inundated the apocalyptic wastes.
Charred porticos replaced by vegete architectural spurs.
Cobalt arboreal broccoli with ivory buds.
The earth as a bowl-shaped altar.
Total dissolution of the imperfect body.
Ablution both anabasis and sepulcher
because we now know what is under Genesis:
the past life of the planet, its demons and its Christs,
Adam pegged to Eve,
                    Shiva-legged, they dance
owl mind, fruit mind, bodies pierced
by harp strings, by the past death of the world:
gutted cities burning in the night, reflected in the black
sheen of a pool out of which, immediately snapped up,
                    an otter crawled.

Birds file back into their eggs. Tomb of the risen.
Uterus of song. Bird-flitted maidens
masturbating to that instant before noon when all walls
fall away and all who have ever lived
commingle, naked, sleepy…

The sensation of being eaten,
the sensation of eating,    the same,
neither dream nor agony
but the storied, sacrificial sanctuary of Hieronymus Bosch
who, having jettisoned divine judgement,
through an edenic-apocalyptic-paradise of wasteland and
    nascent energies,
                    walks toward us,
holding up in one hand a blackened rosary,
proffering some red fruitballs in the other.


        ★★★

# APPENDICES

### The Triptych's Title

Hieronymus Bosch appears to have left us no texts. The triptych known in English as *The Garden of Earthly Delights* is unsigned and untitled. We do not know exactly when it was painted. Guesses range from the late 15th century to the early 16th century. Here is what I have been able to find out about the title's history:

One year after Bosch's death in 1516, the triptych was in the hands of the Counts of Nassau in Brussels. I have not been able to find any documents concerning a title at this time. During the Spanish Conquest of the Netherlands, the triptych was confiscated by the Duke of Alba in 1568 and taken to Spain. By 1593, it was in Phillip II's monastery stronghold, the Escorial. In 1605, Fray José de Siguenza described its subject as that of "vain glory and the fleeting taste of the strawberry or strawberry tree (*madroño*)." He referred to it as "The Painting of the Strawberry Tree."

(Curiously, Caryl discovered strawberry trees on the property of the Rockefeller Study Center at Bellagio. She was told the berries were used for making jam).

The strawberry tree is a European evergreen tree (*Arbutus unedo*) with racemose white flowers and strawberry-like fruit, about an inch in diameter, with rough, crinkly skin, yellow-orange to bright red. The berries are edible, but are also bitter and mushy, and they do not taste like strawberries.

We do not know if de Siguenza invented this title or was passing it on from another source. It is an odd title. The fruit trees in the triptych appear to be apple trees (their fruit is too large in the painting to be strawberry tree fruit), while the picked strawberries appear to be from the strawberry plant (which was not intensely cultivated in Europe until the 15th century, making it possibly a novelty for Bosch's generation), and are, when identifiable as vine strawberries, over-sized. There are only a few. Most of the red fruit in the painting does not resemble strawberries.

At some point the triptych was re-titled "El jardin de las delicias" (*The Garden of Delights*), which over the years has generally been translated into English as "The Garden of Earthly Delights." In this respect, given the action in the central Paradise panel, "The Garden of Otherworldly Delights" seems more accurate.

According to the 19th century German art historian, Carl Justi, who wrote one of the earliest assessments of Bosch's art, the Spanish also called the triptych "*Worldly Doings (el tráfago)* or *Luxury (la lujuria)* and *The Vices and Their End*." Justi thought that The Fountain of Life in the Eden panel "grows from a ball, a giant strawberry, a symbol of earthly desires." From what I can tell, there are no seed-like achenes visible in this cored pink ball with an owl sitting in the aperture.

Fraenger adds to Justi's list of alternative titles, mentioning that the triptych (which he calls "The Millennium") had also been known as "The World's Work and The Wages of Sin." Like Justi, he does not say who was responsible for such titles.

In 1978, the Belgian scholar J. Chailley re-titled it as "Le Jardin alchimique" (The Alchemical Garden).

## Notes on the Closed Wings

Earth disk within sphere emerging from chaos,
the 3rd day of creation         primeval vegetation
  a crystal globe

Upper left corner:
God the Father, in papal tiara,
open blank book in lap,
enthroned in a vault-like space that
mimics the earth sphere

"For he spake,       Emergent earth       "He commanded
and it was done"    cut vertically by      and it stood fast"
                the interval
                between the wings
                (thus division
                inherent
                from the start)—

Flat undulant disk girdled by steamy moat-like waters
  Below: dark hemisphere of the underworld
  Above: sky dome churning with clouds

The vegetal formations on the earth disk are carried over to the interior
panels where, at first at the top of Eden, and then at the top of Paradise,
they become increasingly elaborate and architectural. I shall call them
Terrestrial Transformers. At the top of Apocalypse, they turn into
blackened towers, bridges, mills, against a background of volcanic
flames.

It is possible to experience the closed wings scene as both beginning and
restoration, or as Genesis and Ablution. There is a narrative sense in
which the primeval earth splits open to reveal, from left to right, Eden,
Paradise, Apocalypse, and then, after it has been re-closed, mysteriously
re-presents itself as an apocatastasis.

Words of Walt Whitman pertinent here (from the 1855 *Leaves of Grass*):

"libidinous prongs"

"seas of bright juice suffuse heaven"

"sheathed hooded sharptoothed"

"manifold shapes... the ocean settling in hollows... the great monster
    lying below"

"a hummer and a buzzer there with the rest"

"behavior lawless as snowflakes"

"the ambushed womb of shadows"

"I find I incorporate gneiss and coal and long-thread moss and fruits
    and grains and esculent roots,

and am stucco'd with quadrupeds and birds all over"

"the sleepers are very beautiful as they lie unclothed,

they flow hand in hand over the whole earth from east to west...

they press close without lust... friend is inarmed by friend"

## Notes on the Paradise Panel

Nudes with "pale, flower flesh tones... transparent and weightless as a swarm of white butterflies..."

The dropped, pick-up-stick progeny of Eve and Adam.

Blue and pink, present in key formations and figures, appear, with red, to represent shifting moods of the divine.

The Fountain of Life has here expanded its round pink owl-center orb in Eden into a large blue planetary globe resting (no longer on a nigredo of muck) in a lake out of which four rivers wander. The Biblical rivers of Eden?

"The name of the first is *Pi'shon;* it is the one that flows around the whole land of *Hav'ilah,* where there is gold; and the gold of that land is good; bdellium and onyx stone are there.
   The name of the second river is *Gi'hon;* it is the one that flows around the whole land of Cush.
   And the name of the third river is *Ti'gris* which flows east of Assyria.
   And the fourth river is the *Euphra'tes.*"

Wilhelm Fraenger organizes the "Adam-Eve multiplication" into brides/grooms, masters/novices, betrothed couples etc. To me it seems much more vague and unorganized than that. Blake's term, "organized innocence," reverberates here, but in a different way than Blake himself conceived. For Blake, the terms referred to a synthesis possible after "Innocence" and "Experience." Many of the nudes here seem to be involved with adolescent foreplay. Might we say that they participate in a Boschian "organized innocence?"

Birds, beasts, and fruit/flowers: psychobiological rudders, steering the participants into various poses, combines, dances, nibblings.

Again Whitman, his "Divine Ground from which all things emanate and to which all living things may hope to return."

This panel is Bosch's rhapsody, his "stitched songs." Gestures and con-junctions modulate into one another, as in a waking dream.

"alchemical crossbreeding" –no sexual intercourse (but suggestive align-ments: male nude draped over a huge strawberry, mouth buried in its flesh).

Bosch's Paradise is an East of Eden, a fantasia of an Asia populated by griffins and unicorns, with unpredictable reversals of size: some birds are much larger than humans while others remain naturally sized.

The pink of the Creator robe and Fountain of Life in the Eden panel, predominant in the Transformers at the top of Paradise, darkens to red, especially in the lower section, and is concentrated in red balls, from the size of cherries to that of beach balls. They pop up everywhere, carried aloft by winged nudes over the Transformers or fed to nudes by peli-cans, songbirds, or other nudes. They reappear in transformed guise as strawberries; multicolored "gourds" (which look artificial); over-sized and hollow red fruit which serve as chambers for nudes; apple trees; or various inventive constructions, such as the floating red pod with a red and white pineapple or cardoon crest curving into a thistle-lit transpar-ent globe in which a caressing nude couple sit.

Laurinda Dixon calls these red spheres "the red lapis, the goal of the al-chemical process, also known as the 'elixir,' 'Mercurius,' or 'Christ.'" It is hard for me to think of them as "the goal," since they are part of the im-mediate action, and everywhere.

A variation on the red balls are white dots and pearls which appear to be both decorative and functional. Examples: In the Eden panel, to the right of the albino giraffe, is a spectral porcupine whose quills are cov-ered with white dots. There is pearl-work on the gossamer curtain about the entrance, in Paradise, to the belvedere-like structure that is domed with a round, berry-like, veiled "lookout." Pearls, blueberries, and red berries all spill from the smiling "mouth" of a huge, pink, petaled "pumpkin" (language strains to identify such constructions, as their nameless, many-facetedness stymies syntax; for the sake of a coherent sentence above, I left out the black and yellow stamen-encircled hooked stem, the yellow pimples on its surface, the six long, white feelers, and the nude male consort kneeling by it and caressing it, gaze fixed on the spill).

Many of the bushy trees are peppered with white dots; the iron spikes jutting from the Transformer near the upper right corner of Paradise are covered with white studs. A "caterpillar" of red berries with black dot crests hugs the interior of a curving twig sticking out of a red and white dotted pink carapace flattening someone. Even more mysterious than the white-dotted trees are the patches of tawny earth that emanate white dots, as if the ground were breaking out in a white rash. This might also be projective, remembered from an altered state of consciousness on the part of Bosch himself.

"Men are mortal," Pythagoras proclaimed," because they are incapable of connecting the beginning with the end." Is one of Bosch's goals in the triptych to connect the beginning with the end as a new beginning? Again the possibility of reading the closed wings (once the interior has been viewed) as an alchemical washing, or ablution.

Rimbaud: "It began with a certain amount of disgust and it ends—being unable to seize at once this eternity—it ends with a riot of perfumes." And: "It began with all boorishness, behold it ends with angels of flames and ice."

Might these red and white balls be "building tumblers" in the make-up of life? Medieval sensings of genetic code?

Bosch's stupendous inventiveness plays havoc with any all-over theory. Spontaneous moves abound. Certain figures and combines appear to exist not as ingredients of a planned design but as anacoluthic swerves. Genesis, Eden, Paradise, Apocalypse, and Ablution are all, in part, present in each other, curbing any simple developmental grid.

A film based on the triptych might open with a scene from the closed wings, where muted vegetal towers and supine formations metamorphize into the landscape of Eden. First birds flying about the Transformers, then animals in the dawn landscape, followed by a presentation of The Fountain of Life with the owl in the orb narrating a visionary version of Genesis, leading to a creator drawing Eve out of a sleeping Adam. As the magician-creator "introduces" Adam to Eve, creatures begin to crawl and flutter from the Cenoté, a squeaking, rustling raga-like cacophony. The Trees of Life and of Knowledge display themselves. The Daliesque face below the Tree of Knowledge turns into an actor playing the painter and discussing the grand "multiplication" of the children of Adam and Eve. "Dali" speaks in a watery voice warped by nonsense syllables.

Transition to the Paradise panel could be made via the mer-knights whose armored hordes course its rivers, invoking war and apocalypse. Image of the cavalcade and pool with maidens, voices connecting astrology to mating display. Actors would be naked and dusted, so as to give off a Butoh vibration, humans on the verge of a spectral breakdown. A crowd of nudes enter a landscape bearing all kinds of many-sized fruit, accompanied by huge birds. They move into the "Paradise pose." Cut to the interior of the Tavern of the Scarlet Bagpipe in the Apocalypse panel where a symposium is under way—reflections on greed, sadism, conquest, and immortality. The scene widens to reveal explosions and waste geared to 21st century pollution and war. Musical score using the instruments Bosch depicts, with variations on his music chart.

The screen fills with burning oil wells (reminiscent of Hertzog's 1991 Kuwait footage). A woman's voice meditating on man's obsession with, and the emptiness of, apocalypse. The Fountain of Life slowly makes its way into visual presence through coils of soot and brimstone. Transformation into the watery earthscape of the closed wings, with the Fountain fighting for presence in that which now appears to be a complex mix of wasteland and nascent energies.

### The Terrestrial Transformers

The murky blue forms in the closed wings of the Genesis-scape are the proto-Transformers. They develop, in rhythm with the evolution of life below them, in Eden and Paradise, and burn, as buildings, in Apocalypse. While in Eden and Paradise they mainly evolve from natural to constructed forms, even in Genesis artifice is present. Pods there have cleanly cut openings; vegetation is present without solar light.

The Transformers' implied role in the triptych is one of generating the action that unfolds below them. However, unlike the two Fountains in Eden and Paradise, they do not raise or issue liquid; they appear to be inert. Their human accoutrements caper about, through, around, and on top of them looking like children playing in a park. In three of the four in Paradise, vegetation appears to flourish. The Transformers are the strongest hints in the entire triptych that the source of life is unknowable. A few of them make me think of extra-terrestrial nuclear power plants.

From the lake surrounding the Fountain of Life in Paradise, four streams spread out, three of which pass into three of the Transformers, with one bypassing the Transformer closest to the Apocalpyse panel. As a quaternity, they evoke the four rivers of Eden. But they are not in Eden; two of the rivers disappear inside Transformers; and there appears to be no attempt to express the geographical locations of the rivers in the Biblical Genesis.

In Bosch's Eden, the colors blue and pink are always separate and are not found combined in any figure. In Paradise, three of the four Transformers make use of both pink and blue in their constructions, suggesting a yin/yang synthesis, especially since the vulvic/phallic forms are, color-wise, intermixed.

It is also possible to read the Transformers as the remains of the 3rd day of Creation that persist in the unfolding world of fauna, flora, and human beings—to think of them, especially in Paradise where they are massive, sculptural formations, as testimony to the primordial power involved in the creation of life on our planet.

# Under the Spell of Red Berries

Terrence McKenna thinks that the pear-shaped fruit, lower left corner of the Paradise panel, might be a datura flower, which can be violet or white, and is tubular, or trumpet-shaped, with a 5-angled calyx. Bosch's flower shows 3 sepals (his trefoilian obsession?), and is orange, with dark lavender clover-like décor. McKenna acknowledges that the activities displayed by the Paradise nudes are not consistent with datura hallucinations.

The "elixir" in this central panel seems omnipresent as fruit and creature contact—an osmosis of signs. The word "congregation" comes to mind if we can empty out the institutional and religious sense of it, to evoke a diaspora in pause, a kind of fruiting glimpsed, grasped, in a phase right before ripeness, when the life force swerves toward fulfillment, shadowed by the onset of putrification. In this sense, Eden is the beginning of bud life, Apocalypse the withering. Paradise takes place in that haze of pre-noon, non-torrid warmth. Foreplay as a realm in which the biological and the zoological are not separated out of a mingling that includes the human.

Bosch's Paradise is transcendental because it is a grand rite of participation which includes the painter's own idiosyncratic gists, his metaphoric snips and graftings. While the multiplication of similar nudes suggests that we mirror a kind of eternal human form, and in a Blakean way, are all part of one body, or conjunction, this Dionysian vision, checked by Apollonian aesthetic enjoyment and calm, has not yet moved into passionate overflow.

Or might Bosch be implying that the discrepancy between desire and the fulfillment of desire is never eliminated, since the truest goal of desire is to create reality and not merely to observe it? If so, reoccurring war and ultimately Apocalypse would be the "fruit" of the failure to bridge desire and its creational fulfillment.

A significant number of the human figures seem dazed or passive, I think, because they are just short of aroused engagement and are in a volitional limbo such as I experienced in the first hour of my first LSD experience in the countryside outside of Bloomington, Indiana, 1965. I took off my clothes, sat down in the woods, and just looked around, watching the sun through my held up arm in which I could see the blood flowing. Daphne Marlatt and her husband Alan were one hundred feet away, and I suppose Daphne crossed my mind as I felt up the grass and watched my nakedness with peaceful astonishment. I was in a pause, somewhere between ordinary awareness and an awareness that tipped over into a state in which consciousness was free to pass through anything that inducted it. Or to put it another way: the subconscious, highly stimulated, had become projected onto whatever "scene" it shone on—it mixed sunlight with the blood flowing in my arm showing me directly what I sensed was there. I had become more receptor than actor. Masculinity had taken a backseat to adolescent formations of a wanderlust that was erotic but not erectional or charged.

Next to the pear-shaped fruit, a man releases a bird or salutes one in flight over his upraised slightly-blue hand. He is in a position similar to that of the male nude by the panel's right-hand margin, halfway up, picking what appears to be an apple, Henry Miller, not an orange, in a richly-clustered orchard. Neither figure shows much emotion—in fact, there is something blasé in their faces, especially in the face of the fruit-picker. To his left is another male nude with right arm raised toward a hanging apple. His eyes are closed and his gesture toward the apple seems to take place in sleep or reverie. This state is typical throughout the Paradise panel, even with some of the male figures riding animals in the cavalcade. In the translucent globe attached to the pineapple or cardoon, the female has her eyes closed as if in sleep as the male rather studiously looks at her, his right hand placed on her belly. In the group of men clustered about the giant multicolor blackberry floating in the water near the huge birds, one of them leans his head against the berry, eyes closed, also as if asleep. On the back of a European goldfinch, a male nude dozes, head in hands.

In a number of cases, throughout the Paradise and Apocalypse panels, expressions on both male and female faces are unreadable (in the original as well as in the original size reproduction). I think that Bosch painted them this way, and that such expressions are not changed by surface deterioration. Only three of the thirteen nearly featureless Blacks in the Paradise panel have any expression on their faces (there are no Blacks in the other panels).

So, Paradise is sleepy, or expressionistically obscure. But the panel is less a dreamscape than a psychic reverie filled with berry-gesturing nudes. While there are flickers of emotion here and there, the primary facial expression is nonchalance—these may be the first "cool" people! The male with his butt raised, flowers sticking out of his crack, looks up at "us" from under his arm with no visible emotion. No pain—no pleasure. No concern. His torso is crossed by the arm of a female nude, sitting, with what looks like a bindweed veil over her head. She has half-closed eyes. Her left shoulder is touched by a male leaning forward (with a large blackberry touching the top of his head). He is either sleeping or his gaze is so lowered as to make it seem as if he is asleep.

I can't help but feel that the red berries and their analogues, mainly to be found throughout Paradise, are in some way responsible for the sleepiness and nonchalance of so many of the participants. I count between ninety and one hundred red spheres there (in contrast to a dozen or so in the Eden panel, none in Apocalypse, and probably three in the closed wings Genesis scene). If one adds disks, eggs, orbs and dots to this count, it is as if the spirit or turbine of a rounding drives the triplicating of the triptych. Analogues include petals, grapes, blackberries, openings of tubes and bowls, testicular bags, round towers and the curved, bushy foliage of many trees.

In answer to my query, Dale Pendell writes: "Yep, I see them: straw-berries, cherries, apples. The fruit. There could be some resonance with the nightshade plant—Atropa belladonna (purplish black berries—maybe reddish when ripe), or bittersweet Solanum dulcamara (poisonous red berries). The dreamy effects sound like belladonna—and the nightshades with their tropane alkaloids are the hallucinogen par excellence. That is, seeing things that are not there—especially fantastic, bizarre things. Nightshade was probably well-known as a witch plant—and was an ingredient of the 'flying ointments' (attestations suspect). And one thing that everyone on scopolamine seems to do is to take their clothes off and go wandering about. In the sixties it usually got blamed on acid. Peter Lamborn Wilson uncovered some red berry lore in his book on Irish soma, and speculates that they may be disguised *Amanita muscaria*."

# FOOTNOTES

### "FOLD THE EDEN PANEL TO THE RIGHT"

"A planet spun from dust, rock…": See the chapter "Dust to Life" in Richard Fortey's *Life*, Knopf, NYV, 1998.

**Notes on the Paradise Panel:**

"pale, flowery flesh tones…": Wilhelm Fraenger, "The Millennium / Outlines of an Interpretation," from *Bosch*, G.P. Putnam's Sons, New York, 1983, p. 107.

"brides, grooms, master/novices…": these identifications are to be found throughout the above-cited chapter in *Bosch*.

"Divine Ground…": Malcolm Cowley, "Introduction" to Walt Whitman / *Leaves of Grass*, Penguin Classics, NYC, 1986, p. xiv.

"alchemical crossbreeding": Laurinda Dixon, *Alchemical Imagery in Bosch's Garden of Delights*, UMI Research Press, Ann Arbor, 1981, p. 26.

"the red lapis, the goal…": Dixon, pp. 15–16.

"Men are mortal…": quoted by Fraenger, p. 113.

"It began with a certain amount of disgust…": Arthur Rimbaud / *Collected Poems*, tr. from the French by Oliver Bernard, Penguin Books, NYC, 1986, p. 250.

**Under the Spell of Red Berries:**

"Terrence McKenna thinks…": Terrence McKenna, "Bosch and Yeats on Parade, II," tape from lecture at Esalen Institute, Big Sur, California, August 26, 1993.

Letter from Dale Pendell: the poet Dale Pendell is the author of *Pharmako Poeia* and *Pharmako Dynamis*, Mercury House, San Francisco, 1996, 2003, the first two parts of a trilogy containing a poetic study of botany, alchemy, spirituality, psychology and history.

Besides the materials mentioned in the Introduction, I also read:

*The Secret Heresy of Hieronymus Bosch,* Lynda Harris, Floris Books, Edinburgh, 1995.

*Hieronymus Bosch / Garden of Earthly Delights,* Hans Belting, Prestel, NYC, 2002.

*Bosch in Perspective,* ed. James Snyder, Prentice-Hall, Englewood Cliffs, NY, 1973.

*Bosch,* Laurinda Dixon, Phaidon, NYC, 2003.

*Hieronymus Bosch / New Insights into his Life and Work,* Museum Boijmans, Van Beuningen NAi Publishers/Ludion, 2001.

*Bosch,* R.H. Marijnissen and P. Ruyffelaere, Tabard Press, Antwerp, 1987.

*Bosch,* Virginia Pitts Rembert, Parkstone Press, NYC, 2004.

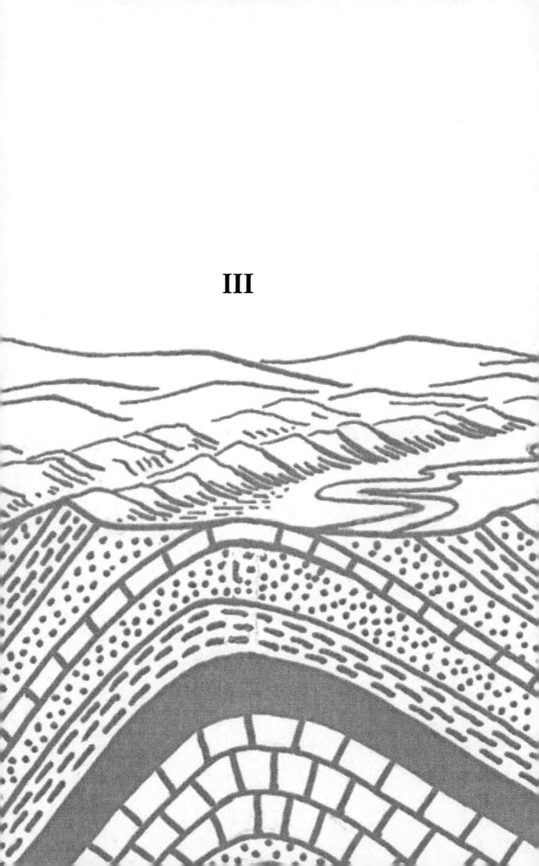

III

## EARLIEST CINEMA

At Cougnac: lopped off stalagmites reveal an ensouled wall—
a group can gather, as in a theater, and gaze!

Combine of uneven wall surfaces, a dozen hand lamps,
a juniper-wicked flickering
shudder-animating the outlined animals.

Wall contours and flutings evoked a megaloceros chest and neck,
thick ibex belly hair, animals partially
submerged, encased imago,
a pupa Cro-Magnon eyes released, in the depths of limestone
there were different kinds of beasts—
wall as screen over which their mental projectors played.

For a fault or contour line to be seen as dorsal
the projection must not only have been titanic
but animal focused, so that one might say
Cro-Magnon was projecting the animal out of his own head
or, ontologically, *his animality out of his humanity-to-be.*

Was this the Fall? The initial soul sighting, or
soulshed between wilderness and culture?

"I am" is animal without animal, a contradiction
*magically* resolved by positing:
the animal that is not there IS THERE.

[December, 2009; written for the *Vanitas*
issue on Cinema]

The horse showing through
the cave wall showing through the horse. Goal
                                of engraving:
to arrive
        As reciprocity.

        ★

A limestone lightning rod for the new mind's animal-
flashing borderless rinks, in-bordered
                            with a line
                        scraped between me
and the thee of cosmic indivisibility.

        ★

The fine sand of creature life poured through the mind's riven mesh.

        ★

In the jigsaw puzzle of creation, the desire to not
just fit, but to allow, through
                    sudden aperture,
the hiss of the shuddering other.

ETERNITY AT DOMME                                    *

Between the junipers flows the Dordogne.
My home is near, as close as gone—
identity in the archaic region of the soul.
Between the junipers flows the Dordogne.

Sunlit crags with chestnuts, lindens overgrown.
What chambers, what cavalcades engraved—
I'll never reach the pillowed rock Laussel arranged.
Between the junipers flows the Dordogne.

Can arrival at yearning's core
be said to decorticate home? Is home my immured
animality, the phantom lurking in my stain?

I'm ancient as never before this afternoon,
charged with karstic urge, fully born.
Between the junipers flows the Dordogne.

[9 June 2007]

# CRAG

La Roque Gageac

Limestone houses terraced up a nearly
perpendicular rise
(hand shading my gaze
as if saluting where the buildings end
and a vertically-
ribbed sun-baked rock wall takes off).

In this rubble-chinked glaze
so many sensations!
Iraq enters my sentences as viral
word insurgencies.
Oil is sign and countersign,
water and oil, the psychophoria of a new I Ching.
"the darkening of the light"
as "the oiling of the waters."

Yet rippling across the surface of the crag,
vectors of spectral baboons,
granular bull-horned snakes…

To feel once again, facing the opaque,
a quiver of birth dread!

Is there a *deus absconditas* in this crag?
(Cave animals as preconscious instinctual structures
brought forth from the unconscious
        out of stone, enabling humankind
to communicate with its unconscious
                rather than
            be ruled by it).

Essence of imagination: uroboric causation.

Was there a period when time was not sensed as part of events?
Does the Cro-Magnon lack of narrative indicate

that creatures and human beings were not embedded in
what we would call "background"?

To look without understanding.
To be penetrated by the observed which enters,
goes on through, without one.

No progress, no damnation, no sin, no pocket zones into which
one can isolate the tidal
coiling in and out of feeling.

Cro-Magnon palm pressed against cave stone.
Equally: absence presence.

Hidden god, are you also the maestro of unfinishable works,
such as myself?

"Don't you see how everything is in mirror pause?
A melody-storied swamp macerated in museum neon...
embrace me. Feel the burned poppies in my fuselage,
the god codicil up my frozen crack."

## COUGNAC, 2007

The mutilated man shall mount the mammoth,
shall mount and
shall enter the mammoth's head.
The man's head shall pierce the mammoth's brain,
the man's head and mutilated body
shall become the mammoth's animating soul
and a lance shall now spit mammoth skull and soul.

This is how we get into animals,
how we project ourselves as versa
into the vice of animal stone.
This is how we lance our otherness
onto the winch of vice versa.

The self,
pupa run through six times, penguin-finned
in its mammoth head
chrysalis.

The self,
a hybridizing amoeba jerking to
its wounds,
peering forth from its mammoth
cradle as if
off the planet's edge.

What a drop
25,000 years compose!
What a Fall
from man exterior to mammoth
to man lodged
mutilated in
this hybrid head.

## ALONG THE VEZERE

Pushed from shore, our canoe traipsed willows, candied firs.

Sunlight, older than lunar girth, cast evergreen cymbals, loosened flails.

The billboard world, the Iraq invasion, radio and center road stripe of
    television:
still as falling shadow water in the back of the brain.

Sky
greenery
water
limestone,     forsythia-bright, pitch-black, serene.

I listened, as my friend, the faun, barnstormed me with a thought:
for every word that presses forth, a thousand, like algae undertones, are
    crowded out.

Crags by medieval post-holes pocked; drooling vines;
river-bends a slowly exfoliating fan.

To find in these khaki-silver ripple-tones a lace, a self-abolishing,
where emptiness twines praise.

Sensations of wildness driving fangs through myrrh.

Pan's sphere! Cruelty, flavored with bane, bleeds from his allure.

Does the Vézère remember antler-bobbing muzzle-hoisted Lascaux
    stags?

When was then? Is now ever won?

Faunal trysts grow archaic in these overhanging fronds.

A "france" before France tinkers with my mental dominoes.

Sky cloud slippers foam with ingot shreds, an exodus lined with plurals.

Heaven? A sky at full speed, mounted slowly on a sword.

Hell? Noon encased, starved of psychopompic peal.

About our final bend:
Minnie Mouse in Spanish Harlem
a bullet-riddled ice cream cone
holding forth...


[for Wade Davis]

## AT THE TOMB OF MALLARME

Death is an erratic too source-obscure to grasp.

At the end of one glacial aisle
the wanderlust of Mallarmé chrysalises.

Black wires bend over his granite cocoon.

In the breeze they tremor,
                    antennify.


                                        [Samoreau, Seine-et-Marne]

# WEEPING WOMAN

[after Picasso]


Excoriated face, fleshed out in rictis.
Out of their lid cups, eyeballs spalling.

Tears, nine inch worms. Knobs of tears on
the spikes of cries.  Dora Maar

flounder-eyed with finger-bitten knotted
handkerchief. Sausage-fat Dora

fingerpillars burrowing facial faults.
The garbage of her face filling with glass.

Whose face is at tug-of-war in my face?
Is it you *Mater Dolorosa?*

"Málaga, how I am weeping!
  Málaga, how I weep and weep!"

Dali's                                                  *
gnarled tree-
knobby
hand gripping,
squeezing the
redness out of a
pod-like tit,
the knuckly bronze
nipple swelling dark ruby before
the blood in the tit
surfaces to
discharge the
nipple:  *Premonition*
          *of Civil War*
                1936

head filled with fetal eyes.
eyes sharing lips.
head helmeted with eyes.
head as a geography of pores erupting, waves surrounding eyes.
there is no part of the head that does not see.
heads with no non-eye relief.

eyes appearing as the only peers, the peerage in things.
eyed & seek, the rills in the face
layered with bird heads, with ferned serpent ends.
with eye vaginal almond floats.
stay! is to girdle as eye bands are to the shuffle of the molting head.
granular disintegration of the tufted fabric of the head.
larval organs dissolving into cream.
say, has that eye apple been spayed?

congeries of eye lines shrubbing into insectile-feelered dark.
thong throng tong-drawn trowel of eyes.
art is to burgeon on its own stem beholden only to
the stamina of its lines.
mine composed of off-shoot eye shafts through which I twist,
accelerating through Unica's fractal beetle,
seemingly designed as a Mandelbrot-set zoom sequence,
in which I infinitely re-encounter what I have just left.

if genes had faces and bodies would they twist like these?
*am* gripping *am,* can't go on will go on,
without centerpole or central pull,
tendril limbs straying into a vanishing varnish roam.
the human configured as part of
the threadwork of
a spontaneous robe of devolving wraiths.

creation as fission. schizogenetic genesis.
no representational nexus.
dyadic primacy of the oldest gods.
gossamer nets to entangle them

so that they ferment, fructify as fruit flies, buried wasp queens,
millipedal elves moving away from each other
yet still attached by saliva strings, lacy scaled vapors
exposing the white, the gleam of never, into which
no one steps twice.

sense of a living midden.
soul as the self buried and mixed with a living Other,
fauna flora particles of an ongoing sentence:
*fullness is infinite fracture.*
totems playfully wavering, as if about to shift
into double helix, to swim into the White,
to perceive, finally, the White Image.

Cannon mouth
window on the void
                    beyond
the railings of the mind.

Wall of axis mundi mouths
stalled, as are we,
facing
           undebriefed
           Lazarus.

Tlaloc as the canvas mother,
"her" black velvet sockets.

Background music for a cobra
erect, wearing a gas mask.

Homage to Lee Bontecou!

Facing a
whirring propeller,
to see in it a snarling dog
camouflaged
fly eye
pulsating
headless cockroach
eye-
       embedded
       bandsaw.

To mate with the warhead
while it is in firing position!

The scaled and loricate lobes of Kissinger's brain.
The horny worms arming his cerebellum.

Albino horseshoe crab bawling in mist.

The gigantic want crowning a breast
—autistic nipple.

The sudden soot ovulation
as blowtorch sperm converges on a macular cavity.

Box jellyfish mind construction:
balls, wires, tiny skulls from which dangle
fanged vanes.

   Aerial
   Boschian
faceship,
   the eye
compartments
emanating
rotary
cicada thrusts.


[Chicago, 2004]

# SNAPSHOTS

Ndary Lo's chains   descending into pans,
 chain-filled pans.
From the sky,   falling,   aligned,
             linked shackles,   Senegalese bone.

From the Gorée Beach, where the *négriers* departed,
chains made of vertebrae   a kind of rain
                that never reaches
             —like thousands chained in the holds—

                ground.

         \*

         Rothko's
      clouds corralled
      as feeling pillows.
Absence squared.
         The terrible squared
right angledom of
             absence.

         \*

Tanguy's *Imaginary Numbers*

   Chains of schizoid stones.
             Glyphic
         near-alphabet
      agloat on mind's
             alabaster.

*

In Breughel's *Eden,*
          ferocity pauses. Eve
reaches for the world-end fruit. Tiger
and adder make eyes at each other.
  A pear tree testiculates.
  Woods, broccoli-tight.
Leaf
chime.     Premonition of
        the anthro coup-de-grace...


*


Dali's cock as a cucumber cathedraled by ants.


*


  Antoni Tàpies has made a bed
for us to eye in,    *La Sábana,*
bed-sheet     kitchen sink
  drained of
        the whole thrown in.

Dead mirror upon the wall,
a waste land is melting in your drawn
       & quartered
    starch.

# A SOLILOQUY FOR HENRI ROUSSEAU

A jungle has displaced my loneliness.

How much I want to be loved!
To be one of the *Immortal Painters*...

Despite my solidity, my caring,
I am a strategic zone of vacuity,
an empty stage on which
the contradictions of society are acted out...

I am a wise person. A palette of magical possibility.

Here I am with my blue jay head.

Here I have become a raven-headed bear.

This evening I am a three-toed sloth, an ecosystem unto myself,
vibrating with hundreds of exoparasites.
Blue-green algae live in my hollow hairs,
I am home to over a thousand beetles!
Once a week, I climb down from my canopy, defecate, and return.
Some beetles leap off of me, deposit eggs in my dung, leap back on.
The eggs germinate. Will the young insects find an Apollinaire or a
    Picasso to call home?

Why do these carnivores always appear,
tearing apart herbivores under my monotonous leaves?

Through the foliage, can Satan be heard snickering?

Here is a solitary oak. With my wife's permission,
I will open its door.

A multitude of ants emerge from a small black purse.

A burning coal turns into a worm.

Animals torn to pieces parade by.

These are my ceibas, my daturas, ah an aspidosperma, a banyan...
these are the trees of my disguise... chonta palm... flowering
    calliandra...
walls of green, walls of summer hibernation...

An anaconda rises vertically from my lake. On the shore
it turns into a beautiful elephant-gray woman, her body tattooed
    with the Garden of Eden.
Has she not sprung from one of my nicest ribs?
But immediately she goes for the tapir hiding behind the momordica...
I watch them screw while she eats one of his warty fruits...

I am like a boy in a studio woods
playing doctor with the force of nature...

a humble man with an argonautic moustache,
an alpha cherub
capable of instantaneous travel
through millions of billions of stars...

Something is always congealing,   seeking
group strata,   full wet skirt,
Gaudi in the cornerless blend of it,
Munch's benders,   released of starch, but   *of* fixation,
opening the locks on
     afterlife   death   this life
pooling,   deboning the polarities,
          poling with Charon in
          blood azure.

"I came into the world as a sick being—in sick surroundings.
My youth was spent in a sickbed; life was a brightly lit window."

César Vallejo: "I was born on a day when God was sick,
                         gravely."

The moon's testicular tube-reflection
transfiguring night's indigo carmine lake.

Waltz with me, lung to lung. "O darling, look!
                              Next to us, a green
larva is vampirizing his slumped booty!"

Sister Inger's speckled dress, splotches roving.

Clasped hands form an oyster-gray vulva against her dead gown.

Moonlight, concentrated in pickets, passes through a woman's face
whose eyes for an instant escape its gangrene drench.

A road boas by a clump of girls on a pier.
Down through brown arboreal reflection
   they stare into the Munchflow.

And what is the Munchflow?  The fetal thrashing of
          those forever unfully born.

A kiss! Her face, consumed, becomes his beak.

Showing through their fused bodies: cobweb-thin cocoons.

> O anima emanating separation!
Away from him she glides toward the shore,
her long hair a telephone wire that cannot be cut.

"People's souls are like planets. Like a star that rises from the darkness
—and meets another star—only to disappear again into darkness—it is
the same when a man and woman meet—drift apart—light up in love—
burn up—and disappear each in their own direction."

The devil's footprints on the bedroom ceiling. Ghosts of the utter
    failure of prayer.

A slimy, soft-horned snail, carrying a brothel on its back.

Pitch-rust river encircling Millie, then Dagny, under Munch.
                    Who called this woman *Madonna?*
She has elsewhere eyes, a menstrual halo, cum-smeared breasts!

"Without anxiety and illness, I am a ship without a rudder."

Stopped on the road in darkness oleaginous as treacle:
    a car with blood-red eyes.

Adam's mahogany penis by a tree trunk radiating fire,
                    whose root metabolism
suckles skulls, crocodilian mulch.
                    Pregnant Eve stands by.
Tree once, with fetal wick, a *burning bush.*

Along  Snow Avenue, asparagus trees are blackening,
        swirled in the caul of a wind
                    boozy with throttled
        valves, aortic hives.

Sister Laura sits locked in perpetual, unanswered, large-eyed pleading.
Before her, a blood flower sucks nourishment from a circular table

whose patterned blood-red cloth
            resembles sections of her brain.

O-shock of a fresh dead man discovering that the beyond
*is* this world oozing through all its pores,
streaks of sky seep through the path
upon which this shocked O holds his head and screams
arched by a sky coldly boiling with the blood of all
who have lived
                    O-scream discovering each
scream is intelligible, the slaughterhouse screams,
the insane scream, your sex opens wide,
rugged candle refueling on gusts,
articulate flame in the trench of your sex,
shaped like a live woman holding
her earless head, her face ocellated with screams,
in each scream the screwdriver of the mind
attempting to loosen the bolt
God sank into it like a pitiless dry well.


                                        [April–August, 2006]

# GOYA BLACK

Text of shadow gore. Cowherds
with leg stumps sunk in mud, cudgels flailing.
Roving colon of humankind.
                              Text
of tunneled pilgrimage. Blind light hangs,
sniffing the mob's expanding hood.
Rutabaga mugs. Bubbling dirty cream:
the flesh of gape-mouth, goggle-eyed anguish.
            Munch sidewinders through.
                        There are Golub
torture hooks rusting in this shadow scrimmage
peppering our own mortal broth.

The son of man's left arm stump
roman candles in Saturn's throat.
The bloody stump of allegiance to fear:
pulp in the grinder of power.
The son of man's legs, pressed bell clappers
before Saturn's trestle bent thighs.

        Lean forward, you witches,
your billy goat god has a butchersome tale to bleat.
Some are hysterically daft. Some
the ground has already half-devoured.
Some sit just giggle-wiggling their toes.
Pig-ignorant urn beings
            clumped by
        night's console.

From a deep well of sand
a dog looks up with supplicator eyes.

Does he see the apparition in the sky Goya sees?

The son of man entangled in dirty bed sheets
    with three old and ugly Fates.
While they toy with his thread, this fool
    is busy solely in his crotch!


[for Jerry Rothenberg]

BLUE SPHINX                                                *

[after Leon Golub]


Shed of eternity—the riddled self
                    poised, tripodic.
            What have you done,
man, with the animal powers
    by which you entered time?


        New Junk Yard dog
            now on the street,
        an American merc
    on dog alert,    in defense of what?
The right front leg-arm, as long as that of a Caravaggio
    executioner—
is that this guy's Las Vegas push, his gambled stability?


Glassy street-dark blue.  An East River serum glint.
Baudelaire in a crew-cut. The merc who bombed natives
    here stuck with the logos of his wrath.


Rilke once slept all night between the Sphinx's paws.
Imagine him awaking to this neon-gangrene-faced merc,
    the freak animality of his radiance.


Condomplatz, where the AIDS-infected pass,
"ghosts by day accost the passer-by"
life on the street, no longer post-Romantic Ginsberg mudra
    or OM-intoning "saint"
or even Manson tarantualizing runaways on filthy rugs.
The oil and fumes of Kali-Ma glint through
            the hoop of self
        ringed with Shiva fire.

# ODE

Daughters Nancy Spero mined through Artaud, plunging
into his Bowlahoola the seminal muscle of her tongue
to release these pater-crusted Rahabs,
to let them strip and restrip
—from pedestal to Golden Lotus—
the binocular manacles from their feet,
to let them ungag their cunts,
to let their cunts stick out their tongues,
to let them dance inside out the accordion akimbo kick,
the dildo trot, the serpentine waver prance,
Ms. Gig and her wiggling tricksters
rotating through the monument blockage, rooted and free.

To no longer be a man but a calendar of sieved destinies.

Acknowledge that you are unknown to your Self.

If your ears could perform, they would peak into scimitar moons.

Self has not become solely human. The flights of rapport between
human and animal realms has never stopped.

Is the human a Fallen monkey?

Eye holes of a crocodile mask,
    empty portals onto
the moonlit gore of the animistic soul.

Bicephalous *nkonde,* back knife-embedded with world rule bile.

A five-armed Rumsfeld Vishnu:
one arm thrashing an Iraqi
one arm salivating
one arm a slot machine lever
one arm holding up a smashed Mesopotamian vase
one arm in buddhistic mudra.

Lion bearing a golden mummy. This loot!
    (Am I an image-looter?)

What is my squawk? In what calabash is my cantata?

What chrysalis is woven through my diadem?

        Crossing
    the abyss:
    ants bearing a locust palanquin,
they are accompanied by Artaud's screams
issuing from a clear incandescent lamp,
    the filaments of which are worms
        emitting light.

Birth gong,
emergent
sound child.

Harp of
a gorilla
haruspex.

Photo of a blind Hiroshima girl, eyes opaque liquid.

Are angels wired with insect irises?

So much silence
composed by Euro-noise
dead masks
their spirits trapped in glass
glass as the soul of the museum
the opacity of glass

Prometheus embroiled in a cinder.

At the top of a funerary post an Oceanic guy buggering a god.

The insides of a saw
in which a one-legged *complete* man is dancing.

Maenad boxing gloves stuffed with paralyzed gophers.

In the labyrinth of a mushroom:
the brain trails and blood fissures of our creator's
prowed drum.

So does the poet, drunk on stone,
pour his siliceous soul into sink hole
ink flows.

What have we taken from the animal?
EVERYTHING.

Atavistic wrath—how to gut it?
Was Hitler packed with crushed Neanderthal gonads?

Loon with a smiling moon carved in its back:
the sealed diaspora of origin's spume.

    Perpetual decentering.
       At Smithson's Spiral Jetty's end:
        dazzling blood-colored
           wastes of sawed-off souls.

Museums: weigh stations of exiled souls.

Bruce Connor has built a screened booth so the zombies
undressing
cannot be stared at.  They strip into red shades,
  vermicular tunneling snakes.
Screen patched with torn black hose, dusty fake roses
—so beauty is not lost,   it is just
    enclosed in a subterranean
                *bardo.*

[Paris, June, 2008]

Ravage red
blistered light of hell
   robe demeanor
timid and tender choirboy
      crosshatched beef of
the blockaded river Soutine felt facing
nature
impacted with Soutine.
                      Broken straps of clinging
meat,   lap this, God,   nuzzle what you've riven. O-
hole of a rabbit's mouth
pit sinister,   next to a giggling
discombobulating
   rose bowl.

Soutine's Great Wall:
tomatoes under squish!
I remember Sanjusangendo
—thunder-scrolled warriors with lightning spears
     *versus*
this waiter pulled askew in sanguine vest.

Turkey in a cloud burst of pus, pearls and wattle breakage,
legs mossed blue    (its red-dotted breast evokes
   the menstrual disks of Le Combel)    hung garroted
black matted feather choker, rack of stiffened claws.

Gladiolas, wind-gusted flags at sea in bowl.

Undulant buildings, Ku Klux Klan blank,
eye holes tarred with introspection's lack.

Anselm Kiefer's crumbled "Sarajevo library" a few blocks away
is tame compared to what hit through Soutine.
Are these trees dreaming in a hurricane
or are they the arteries of a giant having a stroke?

Landscape as immersion urge colliding with the abstract
inner machinery of its parts.

Is Soutine's psyche still trapped in birth passage?
Glazed in uterine trance?
Do these upchucking knolls track forceptal yank?
Whirr of fetal gobble?

Never mined.   Here's some meat
grinning like Tige, Buster Brown's dog.

And here is our Pheasant Queen plucked, recumbent on a urine-stained
    cloud.

Simultaneous creation / destruction,
no correction, *no renovation.*

Combustible rumba of thatched reconnaissance
under Smilovitchi's judgmental stare.

(And yet, we are watched over by a jaunty mouse-eared god
    in floppy tilted toque, a bit daft, half-asleep
with abattoir intentions even he does not grasp
    as he grips
                the red blob we are to him,
    purses his lips   and wrings us out)

# LOOKING AT OBJECTS FROM GABON

Bring me my bag of teeth,
bones & dough,
whistling with bits of skulls, shells.

What else as base?
Marsh on which to establish
calabash power.

Featureless copper face.
Eye organ    button-hinted.
Face of nature, my face
    to a beggar, my face
                to Bush.

Mind puts forth its lotus prongs.

Shovel face.
Wired wall of face.
Where compassion ran, like indigo. Where
vengeance,
            like gleet.   Face
    of militant refusal.

*Totally virtual destiny:*
the ground zero
lightning rod of this aeon.

Let me experience the drill of my consciousness,
the marl of my subcutaneous
        disgust for life under corporations.

Bandzioku spends her days at the edge of the comprehensible.
She is a spirit with a shadow longer than her life.

I eat her iboga root,    find myself,
with shadow surplus, in an ancient barque

where a black swan strummer plucks
bicameral blowback from the inner stereo of rock.


[Dapper Museum, Paris, 18 June 2007]

PARADE

Mr. Wheelhead in top hat with feather-fiery fuse.
He's blind. He leads the parade.

Rolling in place, he's followed by Mr. Tenpinhead,
paintbrush hair, legless
on rusted turned-sideways wheels.

He's got a flag on a tall wire, stiff in no wind.

Childhood frozen like a goofy parade.
Toys as a form of sleep's wheeled yet wooden gestures.

With stump arms too short to reach the steering wheel,
Mr. Gnome is driving the Caged Animal Truck.

Mr. Nearlyalllegs is a white, striped, split pole,
glove hand on a long arching stick.

Each toy a cartoon of our wandering
   Hotel Kendall's lobby, buffet-breakfast bound.
All of us on wheels that don't belong,
all of us shadowed by a tall gown-billowing lady
   thrusting up her parasol. She too is on wheels,
      mouth a smeared yawn.

[Cambridge, MA, 21 October 2007]

# HASHIGAKARI

for Matsutani Takesada


Out of your womb of injury,  a dragon dusted white and pouring,
    gluing your id-entity to the pulsation of your blood.
A ragged black blot presses through the hibernation
        consciousness can be.

Blot or button-like black bubble—
it is the axis of the revolving, fiery wheel
    to which,
            Japanese in Ixion space,
you are separated and bound.

Axis or Motherfather, cleft heart of the first division,
earth separating out of primal black liquidity.

        Coiling through the compromised blackness,
        riverine saliva
                        curling into a lip    filling
        with white blood,   congealing.
        Origin of your struggle to keep
        identity from eating its tail,   from becoming
        fake whole.
                    So, only the gibbous is true,
        only the gibbous radiates irreality,
        the specter of that first division,
        the interruption of black,   the payback for being
            without rupture.

To restrict release to its moment.  No image.

No progeny.   Only a line crossing immensity.

I watched you kneel before the Angel of Annunciation.
I overheard her say:
    "You are to bear the stream-charged material of an emptiness
    ripe with closure. Nothingness is singing its way

through you, a *yoin* vibration, of turnstiles and eggs.
Perhaps only you
hear its whirr of propeller white, of clock-defaced time
being effaced?"

I peeked under the Angel's gown to find
packs of poison toads,   paths tripling
with manticores,   bee kobolds with mead-filled pots,
Pandora and her scorpion boxers,   sheens
    such as no one has ever seen,   dun-vermilion-greens,
    caldrons of natal spleen,   all the ballyhoo that fumes
    below
    the Motherfather's cycling opposites.

Stroked

into amoebic hesitation,  a black oval
called Evolution
    attempting to buckle, to evoke
a pepper with troughed bulges (but black,
note, not green or red, thus a pepper with morgue-
sheen, an ebony idol),

a black oval called Gravity
self-creasing into vulvar folds.

Inside a ghost circle
a clipped caterpillar arching to connect.

What is behind your sudden explosions?
A line curves around, as if to become a lopsided orb,
as it nears closure, as if from behind the canvas,
a huge splat of black glue finishes the job
as if explaining to the poor line
that it was simply not up to the toad body attached,
in whose belly is a golden key.

What have you done with all your unused color?
Has it been left in the mirror room, as piles of masks
    and silk brocades?

Some part of you must still be
waiting to be born. That's good, that's reservoir.
Osaka awakening at the bottom of the sea.
Celliform sprouting tubercles, nodules, a maze of
     mycelioid growth.

Yin
   mish
Yang
   mash,
—art as synthesis
   melee

(Will our white balls ever
learn what our black testicles weigh?)

How bring what is here and what is not
into one?
On a stage?  Not in a mirror room,
     but on a
               Noh stage of the mirror?

Are you also, Matsutani, a peacock in a heavy cream kimono?

     Thick book of our
        single
                 page being
   in the courtyard of royal absence.

Perhaps the origin of your black is in illness.

This wave, where did it start up?  In the mirror room?

Has it a break point?  A spill goal?

Are your paintings
*hashigakari* for events that occur before
and after
the paintings themselves?

Do these "suspension bridges" bear the reverberation of
an elsewhere
relentlessly dislocated?

Paintings as skid marks of an accident
careening out of the mirror room.

Nothing
is happening here. Everything has already
happened.

Tubercular eternity.
Punctured black udder
s
t
r
e
a
m

    collecting, as you may have for eight years,
in a hammock, dripping through…

black womb out of which
your hibernation continues to pour,

a perfectious wound.

Here they come, the more-than-less-than-us,
the toons under us, creatures draped in feathered morn,
in bowlers, stuffed jaguar-tail crowns,
big-eyed skeletons bearing god copal,
Katzenjammer Hero Twins,   Smoking Frog,
Curl Snout with lots of eyeball jewelry,
Jiggs and Lady Xoc
            (pulling Guantánamo through her tongue).

Speech clouds with funnels, grids of glyphs.
Funeral pot rollouts: Maya "comic strips."

Through White Bone Snake Gate,
Sea Hag and Water-lily Jaguar jostle, slice.

One Blowgunner, his nose is phallic, with hot dog fervor.
Over bound Sweet Pea, Bearded Dragon lifts his axe.

Skulls with sunglasses embedded in their sockets,
corn silk flowing from their pates.
Walking tableaus with bloodstained scarves, enema bibs.
Supernatural space is red.

"I am timeless!" the jawless Gump executioner yelps.
He misses Maize God's neck. Ejaculates through his fontanel.

Now, who is that bulb-bellied coyote, ritual noodles
looping his skinny thighs? He's pounding stuff bubbling before his paws.
Was he your momentary escape from the human fix?
Behind him, caked with enucleated eyes,
a jaguar nagual turns his head into a mirror.

Harp of an upturned infant. Have you, as Whimpy,
strummed burgers from that primordial bow?
Only the Jaguar God is intact, in circus mayhem honking his spots.

Chopped up anaconda, stacked into a throne.
A cigar-smoking firefly sambas by a rabbit scribe.
Lopped heads sweep up into the blackness as evening stars.

With goose-dragon power, I sounded my conch
projecting all its seminal Naz, for the Spaniards were right around the
    glyph
knotted in homophobic madness,
shaving their mothers, milking their dads.

Alice the Goon. Stingray Spine Paddler.
Monkey-men copulating in sud pause syncopation, their lips cut back.

Xibalbá: the dance floor under America, under the range,
forever vital in caricaturing us, divining our vows.

Give me your claw bundle, Walt Whitman,
your Maya hypodermics. Let me feel what came up in you
as these gods and lords *milked you, yes, into existence*
High on coffee enema, have you a Thimble Theatre skit for us this
    evening?
Or are you now totally Otherworldly,
a Xibalbá denizen, decapitating any young poet whose neck is not
bandsaw strong enough to dance your blade?

In a whisper, Walt pointed out Dante, a senior male,
sitting on a low branch. "He's an Itzamna look-alike,
balls hanging out, that's his pose—
he has large white nipples,
his toes are extremely fat and huge."

## INNER PARLIAMENTS

Three mahogany men in a four-poster mahogany bed
embedded in a conversation with *Nightwood*.
All turn as self-duplicates of the mind of the book.
They stare from the depths of this
blank page. Every dream is an over-determined plexus
accosted by a Coyote disguised as I. Between dream-self and
these three I-beings is a nearly impassable gulf.
Adventuring truisms attempt to cross,
caked with shamanic effluvia, capsized soul boats.
The forever-daily project: to dump the obvious, to reattach,
to regain *I is* marinated in perception, to find,
fluttering in the vortex of a cloud,
the snow-bunting of the self—
one's infernality, one's celestial sinew.


    ★


The pupa papa wears a parrot headdress. Flitted by glowing
indeterminates, he sits on a gulf raft,
flicking fingers into I. As I assimilates the finger darts,
the papa pupa turns into rainbow after rainbow.
"I is the suffering of light," one hue speaks, and another:
"I is the navel's untold cosmology.
                    Look:
a monkey-headed human skeleton is dancing in procession with
Gladys Eshleman, a
        dead baby Clayton on her right arm."

Gladys's left hand pats the forehead of a jaguar stroking in place toward
    her.
Its neck is wrapped in a blood-soaked diaper.
Its clawed paws lacerate and release concealment from
the mantle of the Ancestor of All Colors
           who wears a headdress of sting-ray spines,
   spondylus valves and gourds.
Inside Her mantle    there is no body,
Instead:    a mobius band in a groove of I-ways.

\*

In a dream, 16 July, 2009, 2 AM, the word "infanite" appeared,

And in this new word's wake:

> "the dream as infant tile
> the infinite as infantile
> in the infant's night the infinite is nigh"

then   "burial waters"

then   "dream censor: Covering Cherub"

\*

I

is an arm with a hand.

How did I first announce self?

In the Upper Paleolithic, it placed its hand on a cave wall,
spat red ochre around the hand, withdrew the hand,
leaving an I-negative on the wall.

Is what we now call art an elaboration of this I-negative,
Kafka's "What is laid upon us to accomplish is the negative,
the positive is already given"?

I-negativity was thus in place 30,000 years ago.

I is a pillar with base and Doric cap, upon which
an I desiring a saintly melt-down would sit and Iolate.

In dream, I-ness unfolds, multiplies, an Ensor parade.

On a clock face, I is broken minutes chasing stolid hours.

In a mirror, I becomes iota (a tittle in the universe).

"I is somebody else." Hey, a good start!

Dots kneeling by a bank of handless arms.

As always, I is looking for a god place in which to bury
the pillage of its rampage.

When I was conceived, what blasted the zygote?
What redialed its cosmic name?

    ★


Self is an ever-shifting mobile of masks linked to masks
as if by rod-like umbilici,
masks shaped like windmill vanes
with eyes like scissor-handle holes,
assemblies Wifredo Lam envisioned as "Personages."

Are these masks puppets on the strings of an angel puppeteer?

Do all I-beings find resonance in a mask of masks,
                an Angel of the Face?

To realize that we are only alive today because Kennedy
                embraced Khrushchev.
The CIA bullet embedded in that kiss.

The poet can have no system overseer, no
third eye at the peak of a pyramid
like a lighthouse beam onto his psychic sleights—
his stare weighed stairway
  descends through
a Self-assembled sylphwork
     of anti-saviorial
        defiance.

Good morning, Max, are you still on the lookout for what has never
   been?

—Of course. The sun continues to be stored on the wrong side of
   disaster.

I arrived expecting to find you robed in red feathers, assisted by a
pregnant hermaphrodite with a chewed-bloody right arm.

—Think of me as the father of scissors.

Yes, or as the great collagist of the labyrinth, cutting and pasting it into a
new bicameral mind in which an identity in the midden of the instant
supplants consciousness.

—The complete man must live simultaneously in several places, within
several human beings. In him a range of people and multifarious
situations must be continually present. Think of me as a hundred-
headed guy.

Or as a nude sleeping in a water-lily harness rotating through a morning
mined of maternal charge.

—Or as a derbied bird-headed man with brains for ass, both hemispheres
having split his pants.

Are you suggesting that external objects have now broken with their
normal environment and that the component parts have emancipated
themselves from it in such a way that they are now able to strike up new
relationships with other elements?

—If mother had not used my crib for stirrups, Herr Rabbit would not
have had to pop the placenta cork to set my fetus free.

Is this what happens to you from staring at stains on the wall?

—Oh yes, blue immobilities, dormant ochres, centrifugal blocks magnificent in their centripetal sway, mummified hornets bursting their shrouds in order to drill into the bones of lightning rampant in a bear! At wing with my vision, I palpate the bowels of solar foals.

But is anything left of the beginning?

—Calcium-brittle flowers press upward. Faunal penetrations course the vineal verdure.

So who are these half-concealed beings peering out of your vitreous pillars and morel-like pipes?

—Sciomantic divinations. I consult the spirits of World Wars I and II. The nascent dead are avatars appearing in a cypress or a stele. Shell-shocked trolls reassembling via my hell-hocked mind. Souls in Hades doomed to re-colonize in floral nests as leaden yet hissing eggs. For "Europe After the Rain II" read: "Europe After the Reign—of Mars."

In these spirits I detect an older tradition, the medieval Persian world of the *Sha-nameh*. Ghosts of Safavid art, the homuncular grotesques of Sultan Muhammed or Aqa Mirak.

—Ah yes, plants as insects caught red-handed in self-fecundating arcs.

I hear you are stalked by beetles decked out in bells.

—As a blind swimmer passing as a wheat grain through the cross-section of a tree, or traveling as a zap of sperm in a contrary will, I made myself a seer.

Is not all artifice including nature?

—Man's temptation is to identify with a single period in time, and to therefore believe that he can free himself from the tentacles spiderfolded in birth and rapture.

Is that why you have attempted to free everything from its shell, from its distance,

from its comparative size,
from its physical and chemical properties,
its outward appearance?

—Only the sewer cricket lockered in Saint Cecilia's uterus can respond
to that. My point was *not* to find myself *and* to counteract any desire for
harmony with tremendous centrifugal force.

And these half-red-garbed, half-naked "goddesses"? They stand like
pupa-forms in the debris of an observational world. One, a queenly
rose-feathered owl, is accompanied by a swan-headed man with a
broken spear. Who are they?

—Where Mars is, Aphrodite is only a shadow away.

Justice will be done, but does the green hand guiding the serrated blade
have a body at stake?

—In every desire there is a skull whose cranium is a womb of flame.

Whose long blue arm is that milking volcano fumes out of nymph
echo?

—I am only interested in that *which saw itself in me.*

Is not all blessed with the desiccate kiss of farewell?

—Here, then, is the secret of my force: while painting with swan's head
hand I relentlessly regurgitate a crop of pigeon's milk into the beaks of
my young.

We must learn how to sound our mental volume without grieving, to
hear our fingers and not moan with our hands.

—And, while watching the pillage of immensity, to see everything as it
really is: without adherence or bond.

## IN DEEP SLEEP DOROTHEA TANNING RECEIVES
## & ACCEPTS THE AWAKENED CLOUDS ABOVE HER               *


The war in Dorothea Tanning,
human wind tunnels igniting, perishing
(By 1954 the early static scenes,
prismatically shattered,
are deliquescent with non-disclosure).

White phosphoric mist of screening mass,
images not obstructed
but scrambled, pyrophoric.

Color as the moods of gods,
ax glints of Ares, Hekate-spongy blacks.
Abstraction acidicly turning bodies into gaseous peat.

Is that a lighthouse?
If so why does it have a shredding infant in its beam?

She drives her fist into the wall of dream.
Miles inside, something clamps about her reach.
Is this the same snakebird angel
flitting about her labyrinth of fist-walled bends?

Not lead changed into gold
but lead and gold mixed from the beginning,
gold in all its plumbing.

"My dearest wish: to make a picture with no exit at all,
    either for you or for me."


        *


I dreamed Tanning was buried to her neck beneath a bat-hung iroko
tree. Like the straw-colored flying foxes, she had feasted on iroko fruit.

In her early painting, *Birthday,* she portrays herself bare-breasted, dressed in a skirt made of mandrake roots. Crouched before her, winged and lemur-eyed, is her spirit familiar (where, in medieval paintings, St. George's speared dragon is often found). She knows the language of the mermaids. She is *consciously* wild.

In the dream, she inquired: "Are you a body or a colorful area of the abyss?"

*

For whom to live if not for one's inner hag,
hedge rider sailing back and forth in boundary-dissolving flight.

What is her goal? A wilderness bewitched with abstraction?
A culture populated by bodies released from anatomical mold?

Bodies with bones gone rubber. Between skin and bone, worms
   with minds of their own,
worms like frenzied violins,
millipedes fringed with metronomic yonder.

Bodies elastic as taffy blown scarlet, golden,
   a butterfly leech delirium,
                      acrobatic fetal swimmers,
   legs birling, all under the watch of a spider-eyed dog.

Dorothea with her dog in a Cythera-spectral Oz.
Form bisexing itself, peas in a pod guild orgy.

Abstract abacus of calculated fury.
Perpetual metastasis. Dream camera inside her body
   shooting through her organs.

What sore is she harrowing?
Why this proliferation of spirit familiars?
Baby-faced lhasa apsos, bear-pawed dwarf in blue jeans,
night-goggled lhasa apsos, head-mufflered dwarf in boots,
orangutang-armed lhasas apsos, gangly white goons,
huge faceless lhasa apso ghosts…

Are they the hundred-headed surrogate of an unborn child?
Are her pendular swings timed by a centaur in labor?

&ast;

    Dream  3:12 AM
            5 January 2009
On the parvis of a cathedral Antonin Artaud joined the two of us.
He handed me a sheet of metal which he motioned for me to shape into
  a shallow bowl,
into which he placed a bouillon cube, boiling water,
to make for this 98 year old Dorothea Tanning,
  some soup.

&ast;

I see you and can say you because my thymus too is blanched with
    savior.
I dent I-ties in order to turn with you cog-wise high in the night.

Your white crescent moon piled with footless, toed babies.
A decapitated Venus bears, as a stand-in head, a manikin frog.
Plunging, amputated, copulating knots, with long arm-stalks jutting.
A child arched with a head of triangulated, crossboned arms.

Around a TV screen, as if in churning roundelay,
blue and peach body-parts tumble,
                  flotsam
in some ontological washing-machine
                    operated by
a fetusmear gripping—is it a lever
  or an eyeball?

Galesburg does not disappear.
Galesburg is a gale-warped mountain
      refashioned as
the vortex of your thinking,
the eye of the whirlpool's strong central suck,
the plethora of near-forms exuding
flesh drift, sludge windings, muzzle fires

—the incomprehensible impregnating everything—
the mind, in swivel, sensing itself several to its argument.
All is aftermath as time embowers primal loss.

Now on your dream wall I see you project a moving still:

    *Ernst Crossing the Styx*

He stares into the myriad shadow birds whispered through
  the prism of the insomniac's mirror.


[December 2008–January 2009]

To cage you blizzard, to purify
your gizzard while disemboweling
the lizard in its bower. To make these millipedal
feelers mill, to pedal eels, white elvers,
or are they elves? If so, turn piranhas on them
to exacerbate any penetralia
which may have coagulated in my rage.

To age you in an instant aardvark so that no one
can identify a figure in my marble reserve,
for the figure is eaten by the ground and the ground
is poisoned by the figure. The hierarch,
Ducoed and lacquered, is pulled down. And all of them,
blizzard-inquisitored
as fractal fragrance, are caged.

To dissemble thus deny any fulcrum in this annexed
dark. An ark? Din of anodyne shadow passengers
entering. An Aurignacian nostalgia
overcasts my spill. Do *they* still have the floor?
Or is image the sand of picture-trillion particles?
                              Palm here
pressed to canvas to indicate: NO WAY.
Or: all ways all at once. Window on
the shattered mace of authoritative majesty.
The crud we've lost is forever active as cadaver molt.

Dribble of cream zigzagging on skates:
O most thoughtless, most thoughtful century!
Bullet-riddled Clara Petacci! Iwo Jima!
Weave oh weave siphonophoric maze!

Blizzard, I lock you into drawn-down freefall
where the moldy straw
as if by Rumpelstiltskin is turned into aureate flares.

Riot of the dead weight in me seeking a monotheistic throne.

To convert umbilical restraint into julienned white tapeworms
whose cut ends arc through my pour.

Not my being, but being's bender as it is bent through me.

What is Garcia Lorca doing here?  And in a blood canoe,
staring across the lake at Munch's melting tomb...

No god will disinfect the rock of my machine.

In the Cunt of the Celestial Crocodile I solarize as a Hadal sum.

# NOTES

### Combarelles

Combarelles is an Upper Paleolithic engraved cave several kilometers outside of the village of Les Eyzies de Tayac, in the French Dordogne. Cougnac, in a later poem, is an Upper Paleolithic painted cave outside of Gourdon, in Lot. For additional information on these caves, as well as many others, see the index in *Juniper Fuse*.

### Eternity at Domme

Whenever my wife Caryl and I lead tours to prehistoric painted caves in southwestern France, we always visit the town of Domme, a bastide crowning a hill overlooking the Dordogne River. All of us stand, we think, at the same spot that Henry Miller did in the late 1930s when, during a visit to the Dordogne on his way to Greece, he made a marvelous statement about the region in ancient times (see pp. 243–244 of *Juniper Fuse* for the quotation). In 2007, standing at this spot overlooking the Dordogne River slowly meandering far below, a mass of contrasting ideas and feelings from my decades of cave research kaleidoscopically locked into focus. Suddenly I had realized my life.

### "Dali's…"

The full title of this 1936 Salvador Dali painting (in the Philadelphia Museum of Art) is: *Soft Construction with Boiled Beans: Premonition of Civil War*. In his book on Goya, Robert Hughes writes: "Salvador Dali appropriated the horizontal thigh of Goya's crouching Saturn for the hybrid monster in the painting… which— rather than Picasso's *Guernica*—is the single finest work of visual art inspired by the Spanish Civil War."

### Zürn Heads

For Unica Zürn drawings, see *Unica Zürn / Bilder 1953–1970*, Verlag Brinkmann und Bose, Berlin, 1998. A more recent collection is *Unica Zürn*, Halle Saint-Pierre, Paris, 2007. In *Reciprocal Distilations*, Hot Whiskey Press, Boulder, CO., 2007, and *Archaic Design*, Black Widow Press, 2007, there are two other pieces on Zürn.

## Bontecou Haiku

For an overview of the art of Lee Bontecou see *Lee Bontecou / A Retrospective*, Henry Abrams, N.Y.C., 2003.

## Snapshots

For Ndary Lo's art, and the art of other contemporary Senegalese artists, see *Senegal contemporain*, Musée Dapper, Paris, 2007.

I neglected to write down the title of the green and maroon Rohko painting. It is, along with the Tanguy and Breughel paintings, in the Thyssen-Bornemisza Museum in Madrid.

The Dali one-liner materialized out of thin air.

The Tàpies *La Sábana* is in the Reina Sofía Museum, Madrid.

## A Soliloquy for Henri Rousseau

After viewing the exhibition "Henri Rousseau, Jungles in Paris," at the Musée d'Orsay in 2006, I purchased *Interpreting Henri Rousseau*, by Nancy Ireson, Tate Publications, London, 2005, which led me to realize that attempts to interpret Rousseau's paintings didn't come to much. So I invented an interior life for him.

## Munch Dissolves

I hear the word "Munch" in the title of this poem as an adjective. I have been brooding about Munch for many years. There is a draft of the "scream" section, which ends this poem, entitled "During Munch," in *Mistress Spirit*, Arundel Press, L.A., 1987. I was recharged by Munch viewing his Museum of Modern Art retrospective in NYC in 2006. See *Edvard Munch / The Modern Life of the Soul*, The Museum of Modern Art, N.Y.C., 2006. I also highly recommend Sue Prideaux's *Edvard Munch / Behind the Scream*, Yale University Press, New Haven, 2005.

## Goya Black

See Robert Hughes' *Goya*, Knopf, N.Y.C., 2004, pp. 379–387, for a thoughtful commentary on the Black Paintings to be found on the 3rd floor of the Prado Museum in Madrid. This poem is dedicated to Jerry Rothenberg whose "50 Caprichos after Goya" is part of a larger manuscript, "Concealments and Caprichos," to be published in 2010 by Black Widow Press.

**Blue Sphinx**

A reproduction of this Leon Golub painting can be found in Jon Bird's *Leon Golub / Echoes of the Real,* Reaktion Books, London, 2000, pp. 102–103. See *Reciprocal Distillations* for other poems on Leon Golub and his art.

**Ode**

Nancy Spero engaged the life and mind of Antonin Artaud in two major projects: "Artaud paintings" (1969–70) and "Codex Artaud" (1971–1972). For a sensitive overview of Spero's Artaud work, see Lucy Bradnock's "Lost in Translation? Nancy Spero, Antonin Artaud, Jacques Derrida," in Issue 3 "Papers on Surrealism," 2005. I see Nancy's Artaud projects as catalysts for her images of feminine release, taken from many cultures and times (including Greek dildo dancers and Irish Sheela-na-gigs), that proliferate throughout her art of the 1980s and 1990s.

**Muse Holes**

This poem is based on fifty pages of notebook entries made during multiple visits to the Dapper Musem, the Branly Museum, and the Centre Pompidou ("Traces du Sacré") in Paris, June 2008.

**Soutine at L'Orangerie**

The 22 Soutine paintings from the Paul Guillaume collection are now in a "power room" by themselves on the ground floor of the Orangerie Museum in Paris. See "Soutine's Lapis," and its Note in *The Grindstone of Rapport* for other poems and articles on Chaim Soutine's art.

**Hashigakari**

This poem which draws to some extent on Japanese Noh theater is based on the paintings of Matsutani Takesada (Osaka 1937–), who has lived with his wife, the painter Kate van Houten, in Paris, for many years. See *Matsutani / Waves,* Otani Memorial Art Museum, Nishinomiya, Japan, 2000, for an overview of this unique painter's body of work. There is a Matsutani painting on the cover of the January 2008 *Denver Quarterly.*

## Xibalbá

"Xibalbá" is the name of the Maya underworld and the site of much of the action in the *Popol Vuh*. For the past several years, I have been looking at painted Maya ceramics, the polychrome vessels often found in the tombs of the Maya elite. Justin Kerr's roll-out photos have enabled us to view these wrap-around paintings as a single "strip," which, with their glyphs, evoke, for me, 20th century American comic strips, with the glyphs playing the role of our speech balloons. Some of the identities and doings of the gods, heroes, hybrids, and animals on these ceramics will probably remain obscure. For me, they are the finest display of New World aboriginal imagination. Michael Coe's many books, especially *The Maya Scribe and His World*, Grolier Club, N.Y.C., 1973, and *Lords of the Underworld*, Princeton University Press, Princeton, N.J., 1978, are indispensable guides to this Maya realm.

## Max Ernst During the Rain

My interest in Ernst was fired by the 2004 Retrospective at The Metropolitan Museum of Art in NYC. I then made use of two books on Ernst to help generate this poem: John Russell's *Max Ernst: Life & Work*, Abrams, N.Y.C., 1967, and Werner Spies' *Max Ernst/A Retrospective*, Prestel, Munich, 1991.

For a few paintings by Sultan Muhammed and Aqa Mirak, see *A King's Book of Kings / The Shah-nameh of Shah Tahmasp*, The Metropolitan Museum of Art, 1976.

## In Deep Sleep Dorothea Tanning Receives
## & Accepts the Awakened Clouds Above Her

See *Dorothea Tanning*, George Braziller, N.Y.C., 1995. In this book, I am particularly indebted to Jean Christophe Bailly's essay, "Image Redux: The Art of Dorothea Tanning." Tanning's *Birthday*, The Lapis Press, San Francisco, 1986, is a marvelous and moving evocation of her 34 years with Max Ernst.

**Pollock Pouring**

This poem is based primarily on Pollock's *1949 #1* (in the Museum of Contemporary Art, Los Angeles).

Concerning the Aurignacians: it was during the Aurignacian period (33,000–24,000 B.P.) that Cro-Magnon people fully emerged. Varied and elaborate tools made of bone began to appear. What has traditionally been called "art" also took place: in the now French Dordogne, crude engravings on stone slabs, including vulvas, cupules, and schematic animals, and in the Ardèche, at least in the Chauvet cave, paintings of lions, rhinoceroses, and mammoths, some done with the verve and precision of a Picasso. In these senses, one can propose that the Aurignacians have the floor—they are, as far as image-making goes, *the floor.*

**CLAYTON ESHLEMAN** was born in Indianapolis, Indiana. He has lived in Mexico, Japan, Taiwan, Korea, Peru, France, Czech Republic, and Hungary. He is presently Professor Emeritus, English Department, Eastern Michigan University. Since 1986 he has lived in Ypsilanti, Michigan, with his wife Caryl who over the past 40 years has been the primary reader and editor of his poetry and prose. He has published 16 full-length collections of poetry, and 10 chapbooks. His first collection, *Mexico & North,* was published in Kyoto, 1962. From 1968 to 2004, Black Sparrow Press brought out 13 collections. In 2006, Black Widow Press became his publisher and brought out *An Alchemist with One Eye on Fire* in 2006, and *The Grindstone of Rapport / A Clayton Eshleman Reader,* in 2008. Four collections of prose appeared between 1989 and 2007. In 2003, Wesleyan University Press published *Juniper Fuse: Upper Paleolithic Imagination & the Construction of the Underworld,* a study in prose and poetry of the origins of image-making based on 25 years research in the Ice Age painted caves of southwestern France. Over the past two decades, the Eshlemans have led 10 tours to some of these caves, sponsored by the Ringling School of Art and Design in Sarasota, Florida. He has also published 11 collections of translations and co-translations, including the poetry of César Vallejo, Aimé Césaire, Antonin Artaud, Pablo Neruda, Michel Deguy, Bernard Bador, Miklós Radnóti, Sándor Csoóri, and Vladimir Holan. His primary focus as a translator has been Vallejo who he has worked on for 48 years. In 2007, University of California Press published his translation of *The Complete Poetry of César Vallejo,* with a Foreword by Mario Vargas Llosa. This book was short-listed for the 2008 Griffin International Poetry Prize and won the 2008 Landon Translation Award, Eshleman's second time to win this award. He was also the founder and editor of two seminal 20th century literary journals: *Caterpillar* (20 issues, 1967–1973) and *Sulfur* (46 issues, 1981–2000).

Among his many recognitions and awards are a Guggenheim Fellowship in Poetry, The National Book Award in Translation, 2 grants from the NEA, 2 grants from the National Endowment for the Humanities, and 2 Landon Translation Prizes from the Academy of American Poets. His writings and translations have appeared in over 400 magazines and newspapers; his poetry has been translated into 8 foreign languages. His work has also been included in over two dozen anthologies, including *Masterpieces of World Literature,* Volume 2 (Norton, 1996), *Postmodern American Poetry* (Norton, 1994), *American Poetry Since 1950* (Marsilio, 1994), *The Vintage Book of Contemporary World Poetry* (1996), and *Poems for the Millennium,* Volumes 1 and 2 (University of California Press, 1995 and 1998). Forthcoming publications include *Curdled Skulls: The Poems of Bernard Bador,* and a co-translation with A. James Arnold of the 1948 unexpurgated *Soleil cou coupé (Solar Throat Slashed)* by Aimé Césaire.

# TITLES FROM BLACK WIDOW PRESS

## TRANSLATION SERIES

*Approximate Man and Other Writings*
by Tristan Tzara. Translated and edited
by Mary Ann Caws.

*Art Poétique*
by Guillevic. Translated by Maureen Smith.

*Capital of Pain*
by Paul Eluard. Translated by Mary Ann Caws,
Patricia Terry, and Nancy Kline.

*Chanson Dada: Selected Poems*
by Tristan Tzara. Translated with an
introduction and essay by Lee Harwood.

*Essential Poems and Writings of Joyce Mansour:
A Bilingual Anthology*
Translated with an introduction by
Serge Gavronsky.

*Essential Poems and Writings of Robert Desnos:
A Bilingual Anthology*
Edited with an introduction and essay
by Mary Ann Caws.

*EyeSeas (Les Ziaux)*
by Raymond Queneau. Translated with
an introduction by Daniela Hurezanu and
Stephen Kessler.

*The Inventor of Love & Other Writings*
by Gherasim Luca. Translated by Julian
and Laura Semilian. Introduction by
Andrei Codrescu. Essay by Petre Răileanu.

*La Fontaine's Bawdy*
by Jean de la Fontaine. Translated with an
introduction by Norman R. Shapiro.

*Last Love Poems of Paul Eluard*
Translated with an introduction by
Marilyn Kallet.

*Love, Poetry (L'amour la poésie)*
by Paul Eluard. Translated with an essay
by Stuart Kendall.

*Poems of André Breton: A Bilingual Anthology*
Translated with essays by Jean-Pierre
Cauvin and Mary Ann Caws.

*Poems of A.O. Barnabooth*
by Valéry Larbaud. Translated by
Ron Padgett and Bill Zavatsky.

*Preversities: A Jacques Prévert Sampler*
Translated and edited by Norman R. Shapiro.

*The Sea and Other Poems*
by Guillevic. Translated by Patricia Terry.
Introduction by Monique Chefdor.

*To Speak, to Tell You?*
Poems by Sabine Sicaud. Translated by
Norman R. Shapiro. Introduction and notes
by Odile Ayral-Clause.

## forthcoming translations

*Essential Poems and Writings of Jules Laforgue*
Translated and edited by Patricia Terry.

*Essential Poems and Writings of Pierre Reverdy*
Translated by Mary Ann Caws and
Patricia Terry.

*Furor and Mystery & Other Writings*
by René Char. Edited and translated by
Mary Ann Caws and Nancy Kline.

*I Want No Part in It and Other Writings*
by Benjamin Péret. Translated with an
introduction by James Brook.

*The Big Game*
by Benjamin Péret. Translated with an
introduction by Marilyn Kallet.

*A Life of Poems, Poems of a Life*
by Anna de Noailles. Translated by Norman
R. Shapiro. Introduction by Catherine Perry.

## MODERN POETRY SERIES

*An Alchemist with One Eye on Fire*
by Clayton Eshleman

*Anticline*
by Clayton Eshleman

*Archaic Design*
by Clayton Eshleman

*Backscatter: New and Selected Poems*
by John Olson

*The Caveat Onus*
by Dave Brinks. The complete cycle,
four volumes in one.

*Crusader-Woman*
by Ruxandra Cesereanu. Translated
by Adam J. Sorkin. Introduction by
Andrei Codrescu.

*Fire Exit*
by Robert Kelly

*Forgiven Submarine*
by Ruxandra Cesereanu and
Andrei Codrescu

*The Grindstone of Rapport:*
*A Clayton Eshleman Reader*
Forty years of poetry, prose, and
translations by Clayton Eshleman.

*Packing Light: New and Selected Poems*
by Marilyn Kallet

*Signal from Draco: New and Selected Poems*
by Mebane Robertson

### forthcoming
### modern poetry titles

*Concealments and Caprichos*
by Jerome Rothenberg

*Curdled Skulls: Poems of Bernard Bador*
Translated by Clayton Eshleman and
Bernard Bador.

*from stone this running*
by Heller Levinson

*Larynx Galaxy*
by John Olson

*Present Tense of the World: Poems 2000–2008*
by Amina Saïd. Translated by Marilyn Hacker.

*Exile is My Trade: A Habib Tengour Reader*
Translated by Pierre Joris.

## LITERARY THEORY / BIOGRAPHY SERIES

*Revolution of the Mind:*
*The Life of André Breton*
by Mark Polizzotti. Revised
and augmented edition.

## WWW.BLACKWIDOWPRESS.COM